Rants, Riffs and Roars

We gratefully acknowledge the financial support of the Canada Council for the Arts, the Government of Canada through the Book Publishing Industry Development Program (BPIDP), and the Government of Newfoundland and Labrador through the Department of Tourism, Culture and Recreation for our publishing program.

Cover Design by Paddy Moore
Layout by Joanne Snook-Hann
Photography by Travis Parsons
Printed on acid-free paper

Published by
CREATIVE PUBLISHERS
an imprint of CREATIVE BOOK PUBLISHING
a Transcontinental Inc. associated company
P.O. Box 8660, Stn. A
St. John's, Newfoundland and Labrador A1B 3T7

Printed in Canada by:
TRANSCONTINENTAL INC.

Library and Archives Canada Cataloguing in Publication

Stapleton, Berni
    Rants, riffs and roars : the world according to Berni Stapleton.

ISBN 978-1-897174-44-9

1. Canadian wit and humor (English). I. Title.

PS8587.T3239L39 2009   C813'.54   C2009-900404-6

Rants, Riffs and Roars

The World According to

Berni Stapleton

kiLLick press
an imprint of Creative Publishers

St. John's, Newfoundland and Labrador
2009

"My psychiatrist wants me to get in touch with my inner child. I told him I'm from Newfoundland. I was raised on salt beef, salt pork and salt fish. If I've got an inner child he's pickled by now."

This book is dedicated to my mother,
Geraldine "Jade" Stapleton.

Centre of the Universe

When you are first told you are ill ("told," because up until now the fact has only been a suspicion or a feeling or a pool of denial resting around your heart) you can be forgiven for thinking that now you are *the centre of the universe*. It's an understandable delusion.

The first of many.

You are not going deaf. You can be forgiven for thinking you have gone deaf on top of it all because people whisper around illness. It's not your fault you can't hear what they're saying. You will see their lips moving, but you can't hear them because the words stick in their throats. They choke. You will have to do the Heimlich maneuver on them.

Now that you are sick you are suddenly privy to everyone else's intimate medical history, whether you want to be or not. Your illness is now your identity. You are now the one with cancer, the one with the heart condition, the one "with." It's how you will be introduced at cocktail parties. "Hi. How are you? I heard about your condition. I've got shingles myself. That's Harold over there, he's a diabetic. His third uncle twice removed has MS. So does his sister, they're riddled with it. There's Frieda, she's a triple bypass and that guy over there is Ignatius. He's only got one leg, but that's OK, he's only ever had one leg so he doesn't miss it. Get him to show you where he had his gallbladder taken out through his belly button. There's Hannah. She's had her breast off but I don't know which one. Her husband stayed with her too. What a saint. And there's poor old Sooze. She swears there is not one thing wrong with her. That's not normal."

The things people will say. You've got just what my Aunt Sadie had, God rest her soul. What odds if you're sick, you could get hit by a bus tomorrow. Your johnny gown is on backwards.

You are scared, sick (so you are told), needy, concerned for your loved ones, concerned for your not-so-loved ones, concerned for yourself. Now that catastrophe has struck, you believe you are *the centre of the universe,* and you will get everything you need when you need it. But after time spent coming and going and only ever getting halfway anywhere, and only getting half of what you need, and only being able to give half of what everyone else needs from you, you will have an epiphany.

It could happen one day when you're feeling very nauseous and tired and your hair is falling out in inconsiderate little clumps, and you've been dumped in some waiting area in the hospital to have an X-ray (and that's just what you need to cheer you up, another dose of radiation). You've got a nagging suspicion that the powers-that-be have forgotten all about you because you've been waiting now for three hours. You're hoping to God that you don't look as bad as everyone else. They're hoping to God they don't look as bad as you. Your rear end is hanging out of a johnny gown that's three sizes too small, made out of paper, with the strings ripped off. You're wearing your oldest pair of underwear (because who has time to do laundry anymore) and these particular panties have got no elastic at all left in the waist. They're left over from a set your mother gave you for Christmas twenty years ago with the days of the week printed on them. This pair says Monday, except today is Wednesday. You don't know which is worse:

that people will think you've had them on since Monday; or that they'll think you no longer know what day of the week it is.

And both things are true.

So there you wait, hoping for the latest modern medical technology to make you well again, as you slowly realize that all the magazines in the place are ten years old, and you don't want to think about that too much. The woman next to you looks like she's been waiting since 1988. The janitor comes in to mop the floor and gets a perfect view of the scenery up your johnny gown. Your kids will be getting home from school soon, there is no food in the house, and somewhere, somewhere in the middle of all that you will realize that even though you are sick, you are not *the centre of the universe*. A tremendous weight will lift from your shoulders.

You will tell everybody to frig off.

Someone else can be *the centre of the universe*. "Frig off" will become your mantra. Frig off frig off frig off. This is called Frigging Therapy. It feels good. It's easy. It boosts your immune system. But, be warned. When others see you having a splendid time telling the world to frig off, they will encourage you to seek help. Don't do it. Tell them to frig off.

Maid Like Me

"Where's your bonnet?" That's all I hears out of her.

"You got to have a bonnet." I got neither bonnet. "You got to have a bonnet." I don't want neither bonnet. "I don't care what you wants or don't want. Get your bonnet." I lost it. "You never." The dog ate it. "Liar." The wind took it. "Fibber." It fell in the pond and a frog sat on it. "Oh me nerves." I woke up in the middle of the night and the old hag had it on. Sitting on me chest she was, with one tooth hanging out of her head, and a wart on her nose with a big grey hair growing out of it, and she was cackling away, twirling my bonnet strings, laughing at me. And then she floated right up through the ceiling and took me bonnet with her.

She says she's going to wring my neck. I'd like to see her try. Tillie Noseworthy. No older than me and flouncing around like she's a lady just cause she's married to Old Man Winters. She can call herself Mrs. Winters but she's nothing only Tillie Noseworthy who was the maid before me. Thinks she's something, right full of herself, up from Jacques Fountaine, showing off her black hair. She never had to wear no flipping maid's bonnet. I don't see why I got to. I got nice hair, too, nice and yellow.

She don't even know how to lay out fish. Telling me to put the meat side down.

"Put the meat side down." You puts them face up in the morning. "What side of the fish is the face on?" Face up. "But the face is in the middle." I don't mean the actual face. I means, you know, put the right side up first. "But how do you tell the right side from the left side?" What, did you never see a fish before? I never had to dry no fish before but I can turn them over and put them meat side up. My fish don't get no sunburn.

They got a outhouse. No more split-fork drawers. Letting the wind get at me prune. No fish looking up me legs. They might be dead but they still got eyes.

She thinks she's better than me just cause I'm from Boat Harbour. I boards in with them in exchange for which I looks after their garden, and I looks after his youngsters from his first two wives cause Tillie hates them. I does all their laundry, does their dishes and does all their cooking. I works from early morning inside the house until just before sunrise, then I goes down to the beach and works there all day long, youngsters with me and all, until it gets dark, and then I goes back to their house and puts that to rights and in return I gets me room and board. I gets to have molasses on top of me bread whenever I wants. He said I could. I got to share me bed with the upstairs maid. She sleeps downstairs with me. So, she might be a upstairs maid in the daytime but when she goes to sleep she's a downstairs maid. Ha ha. Her name is Verily. She says her mother got it out of the Bible. She says her name is all over the Bible. "Verily, Verily, I says unto you." So what. She still got to sleep with me out in the pantry what used to be the winter kitchen. I don't know what her mother was thinking.

Tillie called me a strumpet behind the old man's back, just 'cause he said I could have molasses on top of me bread. She got some nerve. I wouldn't give her the satisfaction of asking her what the flip is a strumpet. I never heard tell of it. Where would someone come up with a word like that, I wonder? It sounds foreign like. I think a strumpet is, like, a musical instrument. An ugly one. I'll strumpet her. I'll strumpet her all the way down to the beach and back. Who do she think she is, waltzing all over town calling people by strange words?

He's all right, though. Comes home from the store, has a mug-up and a wash-up and then he's gone again. Gave me a peppermint knob my first day. I don't think he'll be a bother. Not like what I went through in Boat Harbour. The Pritchards drove me out 'cause they said I was making eyes at their son. Him with big poppy eyes on him like an old billy goat. Only had a wash once a month. It was him chasing me around night and day, and his father, too. It wasn't safe to go to bed at night. I'm glad to be clear of the works of them.

I gets one afternoon off a week here. Tillie says I got to put it to good use, but what I does is none of her beeswax. There's no end to the tea and bread and jam. They has parties. They had a birthday party for his oldest girl by his first wife. At the end of the party she opened all her presents. She got all kinds of new ribbons, and real buttons, and material for two new dresses. Me and Verily served and watched her primping and preening, and they even got a mirror that we were allowed to take turns looking into. That was the first time I ever saw meself proper and I think I would like to see meself again. They gave out peppermint knobs to their guests and served the butter I made on their bread. The old man says it's better than store-bought. I wish he'd stop being so nice or else Tillie will have me pinched to pieces.

I likes their kitchen. They got an icebox. The ice don't melt cause they puts it in the box with sawdust. They got real glass on the windows. Even the Pritchards had tarpaper on mine. Here they keeps the stove warm all day long, and all night, too, cause the second wife used to catch the chills. I has to get up in the middle of the night to put the junks in it. They got chamber pots up in underneath all the beds. I could do without that. How lazy can you be if you can't walk out to the outhouse? Tillie says it's a wonderful comfort for her now that she's in the family way. As nice as it is to be able to do your business inside where it's warm, it's still me who gets to dump it all out and clean them chamber pots all up.

He got a timepiece. He let me look at it.

"It tells you what time of day it is." How do it do that? "It talks to you." It do? "You put it by your bed and it whispers what time it is into your ear every fifteen minutes." When will it talk? "Oh, well, let me see. Should be soon. Should be right now as a matter of fact. Just listen."

Tillie had a big laugh off me with my ear to the timepiece waiting for it to talk. But he didn't mean it to be nasty. He was only codding around. You looks at the timepiece and reads the numbers. I heard tell of reading words but I never heard tell of reading numbers. Numbers looks funny. Must be some nice to look at a timepiece and know right away what time of day it is. I wasn't going to ask how the timepiece knows if it's two o'clock in the afternoon or two o'clock in the middle of the night. I wouldn't give Tillie the satisfaction.

In Boat Harbour they made me take in laundry from three different places. They took the money for it. I had to get one lot of clothes, scrub it, and put it in to soak. Go get the second lot of clothes. Take lot number one out of soak, wring it out and hang it on the line. Then scrub the second lot and put that in to soak while I went to get lot number three. Rich folks are too clean. Tillie expects me to wash the tablecloth if it's only been used once. I don't. I turns it over. She got tablecloths galore. One for ordinary days. One for Sundays. One for parties. One for Christmas. That's a sin for her. Eating off of the tablecloths belonging to the two dead wives. Tillie Noseworthy. She better watch out. She might be wife number three, but before that she was only a maid like me. And his wives don't seem to fare too good in childbirth.

I threw the flipping bonnet over the wharf. The wind caught it and it danced out over the water. I'm having extra molasses on me bread tonight. He don't mind.

Bride

It used to be one time a person could look forward to taking a plane trip. It was an unlikely thing to be doing. It was a once-in-a-lifetime event. Like getting married. Nowadays you're taking your life into your hands climbing aboard a plane. Taking it into your own hands and passing it on over to the cosmic baggage handler. People still do it, though. They still fly. People go around flying and getting married all the time. Every time you turn around someone is at one or the other. Or both. Sometimes both at the same time. Either way you're brazen. Thumbing your nose at gravity. Trying to get ahead of yourself. Hoping that the little patches of turbulence are only tiny bumps you'll forget by and by.

William wanted a small wedding. A few minutes in front of a judge and a pint afterwards down to the bar. Oh no, says I. This is my once in a lifetime event. We saved up for a year so I could have the whole works. My big dress. My big cake. William is an accountant. He doesn't have barrels of money on him, although lots think he had a whack of it left to him when he was a boy and his parents were murdered by that prostitute that time. He was always hindered by the terrible tragic past. I told him: I said, William, I forgive you all that business. And like he said back to me, he said: many wouldn't.

The reception was not what anyone expected. There was drinking. There was dancing. There was weeping. We ate the big cake. I wrapped up pieces of it in Saran Wrap. Put it under your pillow, you'll dream about the person you're going to marry. I've got a piece for to put under my own pillow saved in my purse.

William hates to fly. It's like he said to me, he said: Sailing through the air in a tin can at thirty thousand feet isn't natural. He said: You'll never catch me on a plane. I made no bones about it. I told him, I said: William, it's no odds to me. I forgive you. And like he said to me, he said: Many wouldn't.

My dress was especially designed and made for me by Geneva AuCoin who lives down the shore. She's got French blood in her. Plus, she subscribes to *Vogue* magazine. She can sew anything you could dream of. All she has to do is look at a picture of it. The lace was flown in from St. John's. This lace has had exactly two plane trips now, counting this one. That's one more than me. The silk came from out of the attic. It used to be an old dressing gown belonging to my Nan. The buttons are real pearls, came off a necklace belonging to William's poor mother. She was wearing it when… you know.

My name is Bridey. Bride, they call me. Always a bride, that's me.

I'm never taking off my wedding gown. I will be Bridey the Bride for the rest of my days. At least I got to walk down the aisle in it. Even if it was down the aisle of the plane. Following William's casket up through the church doesn't count. I don't care what anyone thinks. The dresses were made. Why wouldn't I have my eight bridesmaids and four flower girls there? The photographer was already paid, so I went ahead with the pictures, before they closed the casket. William looked better than he ever did in real life. Death gave him a stern hint of that which he lacked before. And then I had the reception and there wasn't a crumb left. People eat more at a funeral. Stuffs up the big hole they feel in their gut.

We could have been married already and off on our honeymoon long ago. If I hadn't wanted to wait, William wouldn't have contracted the horrible meningitis. Now I've got to fly off on my honeymoon by myself.

William was afraid of what might happen if he got on a plane. He told me. He said he might come down with Airplane Tourette's Syndrome. Just thinking about being on a plane trip made him want to blurt out inappropriate things. Words like: Bomb. Hijacking. Crash. We're going down, we're going down.

When he was taken ill on the eve of our rehearsal supper, I told him. I said: William, now buck up. Get up out of it and I'll forgive you all this carrying on. And he said to me, he said: Many wouldn't. The next night he was worse again. And there was me having to host a sit-down supper with real champagne for twenty all on my own. I toasted myself over and over. And we raised many a glass to William. It's nothing, I told everyone. A bug. The next morning he was deader than a doorknob and less useful. I poked him. I prodded him. I raged. I screamed. Where are the damned rings? I cried.

I kept the wedding gifts. William wanted me to have fine things. He had the best years of my life. I should have something to show for it. All I've got left in this world: Two plane tickets to Florida. He died very peacefully. Except for the meningitis. He did piss and moan a bit, but underneath all of that I knew that he was grateful and happy to see me going on with all our plans like nothing was wrong. Like we had all the time in the world left.

I've had everything he promised. Except the wedding. Now *that* is unforgivable. There's nothing left to do except fly to Florida and eat and drink and dance until I fall down. I will honeymoon endlessly with myself. I'm not giving him any tears. Not one drop of salt. Jilted at the altar in such a spectacular once-in-a-lifetime final way. Upstaged by death. He sails through the air in a Christmas cookie tin at thirty thousand feet, deader than dead in the overhead bin. Flying at last. Now I'm the one with the terrible tragic past who waits to be forgiven. And I know, many won't. Tonight I'm going to put my little piece of wedding cake under my pillow and I hope I dream about him. Me and him defying gravity. Swanning through the air. Holding hands. Thumbing our noses. Going down, going down.

Look at Her

Look at her. Look at her. Look at her. She thinks she's something. She thinks big of herself. I know now she doesn't think she's special. Just because she's famous. Ha. She's not *that* famous. She's only semi-famous. Not even semi-famous. She's only semi-semi-famous. Half of semi-famous. And she's poor. Bet the world doesn't know that. She's poor and she's loaded, ha ha, not loaded rich, loaded drunk. What's the point of being famous or semi-famous or even semi-semi-famous if you're poor?

Look at her. Look at her. It's twenty below. It's raging. It's not even garbage day. Monday was a holiday so garbage day is tomorrow. Anyone with any sense knows that. Look at her. Outdoors in her pajamas, which do not match. That bottom does not go with that top. That top is not even a real pajama top. It's a ratty sweater with holes in it. A blue sweatshirt with holes in it worn over green pajama bottoms. She is breaking one of the cardinal rules of colour co-ordination. Do not test me on the cardinal rules of colour co-ordination because you will lose every time. That is what I tell the universe. Do not test me.

Anyone with any sense knows the cardinal rules. There are things in the universe that should not be questioned. God made the world in seven days. The sun is yellow and goes up and down once a day. Plaids and prints do not go together. The ocean is blue because of the grace of God. Pink and orange do not go together. Stripes do not go with opposing stripes. The problem with all the weather we are having these days is because people are up in the universe flying around in spaceships and mixing different kinds of air around that ought not to be mixed. And, blue and green definitely do not go together. Blue and green ought never be seen.

Look at her. Hauling out the trash in a twenty-below gale in her pajamas when it's not even garbage day. The wind will have it blown all over God's seven-day creation. All over my front lawn. It will fly up and down the street. I expect she doesn't have any more room in the house for all those wine bottles. This is all I need. To look out my front window and see her garbage dancing footloose all over my rock garden. Her garbage. I'd better warn the garbage man. Glass in the garbage bags again.

I like wine. I've got nothing against wine. I've got no argument with people who drink wine, but she only gets away with half of what she does because people know who she is. What gets on my nerves is how certain people can come home all hours of the night and fall out of taxis. What gets on my nerves is how taxi drivers help people up the front steps and into the house just because they're semi-semi famous. She needs her roots done. I would rise up out of my deathbed and drag myself to the beauty parlour if I had roots on me like that. I would not be caught dead. I would climb out of my coffin if anyone tried to bury me with regrowth like that. I wouldn't rest in peace at all with a head of hair on me like that. She is breaking a cardinal rule. A woman's roots should never be more than two shades lighter or darker than her dye. Red hair is not her colour. Look at her. It's eleven o'clock in the morning. I can see right through those pajama bottoms. I've been up since seven a.m. I've got better things to do than lounge around in bed till all hours with a hangover and then put the garbage out on the wrong day. My hair has been washed and set and dried and teased and sprayed and styled. My hair does not move unless I tell it to move. I tell my hair: don't test me. If I sleep on it just the right way without moving it lasts a week before I have to do it again. My roots are perfect. My makeup is done. My nails match my lipstick which matches my skirt and my shoes. If God, in His infinite wisdom, strikes me down dead today I will march into the light with the utmost of confidence. I will greet eternity with the utmost of serenity. God will take one look at me and know that I am a woman who takes care of herself. God will appreciate a real woman like me who invests in Merle Normal and Estee Lauderdale for her skin care. God will appreciate the fact that I have walked for thirty minutes on my treadmill and had my Weight Watchers breakfast. God knows that I know which day is garbage day.

She'd better not come knocking on my door again if she locks herself out of the house. That would be just like her. Put the garbage out on the wrong day, lock herself out of the house and then come knocking my door, asking to traipse through my home, dripping slush all over my Swiffered floor. Wanting to go out the back and climb over the fence and break in through her own basement window again. That just gives hooligans ideas. What if a hooligan sees her breaking into her own house and then decides to break into *my* house? My fence is on a tilt from her climbing over it all the time. Why does *she* get to be half famous? I'm the one who flew to Florida in my wedding dress. I'm the one who suffers with the tragic past. Getting her picture all over the TV and in the papers just because she goes around doing benefits and fundraisers all the time. She's got no business doing benefits and fundraisers. She hasn't got two cents to rub together, not judging from the state of her house. She's not even very funny. She's not funny at all to talk to. She's not anything like you think she is. She's not anything like you think she's going to be when you see her up on stage. Up on stage is one thing, but then when you talk to her it's like there's no one there. It's false advertising. The way you think she's one thing and she turns out to be another thing. There is a cardinal rule about that. People are only allowed to be one thing. One thing. No going around being this thing and that thing depending on where you are. That gives false impressions and leads to letdowns. The only reason she is funny on stage is because she writes down the lines ahead of time. Anyone can write out funny lines ahead of time. If I wrote down one-third of what comes out of my mouth, then I would be funny on stage, too. Except I wouldn't need to write anything down. I am naturally very funny. My friends are always laughing at me. Who can laugh at her, though? Not me. Not with the stress of worrying about whether she's going to lock herself out of the house again. Or if she's going to fall down in the snow in her pajamas and freeze to death. There wouldn't be a snowbank in front of her house if she'd get up at a decent hour and shovel the place out. I suppose she thinks she doesn't need her driveway cleared just because the bank came and took away her car. There's no need to let the place go to the dogs. She says she sold the car but I know the bank took it because I talked to Ida, who talked to

Grace, who talked to the gambling addict down the street who has a daughter who used to work at the bank before that embezzlement thingy. Look at her. If she'd mind to take a look around she'd notice that no one else has his or her garbage out. This is what is wrong with the world today. People won't take garbage day seriously. She doesn't take garbage day seriously. She has no sense of responsibility. I phoned her five times yesterday and she did not call me back. Not even once. I left four messages. Normal people pick up the phone every once in a while. Normal people answer the phone. Normal people make phone calls all on their own without needing to be reminded. I wanted to tell her about how I went to the drugstore and the woman who does the makeovers at the tester counter wouldn't lay a finger on me. "I can't improve upon perfection," she said. "*You're* the one who should be teaching *me* a thing or two," she said. I had a like to die. God knows I am not one to understand why so many people like to make a fuss about my appearance.

Part Two

What are you doing?
Hi.
Give me your hand.
No, I'm good.
Good and frozen.
I slipped.
You've got nothing on your feet.
I lost my slippers.
I'll get you in the house.
I've locked myself out.
That's no reason to be lying in a snowbank.
I'm trying to think.
We'll go to my place.
I don't want to be a bother.
I just happened by coincidence to be looking out the front window at the exact same moment you went down. Thank God I'm right next door. If I had to drag you any further than that we'd both perish.
I like your coat.
Thank you.
And your hat.
I love purple.
And your gloves match.
Well, you didn't expect me to rush right out into a blizzard with nothing on me, did you? There are cardinal rules.
Everything goes together.
I have to let go of you for a second to unlock the door.
Why did you lock the door?

There's nothing wrong with locking the door as long as you've got the key with you so you can get back in. A person can never be too careful. Stand on the mat so you don't drip on the hardwood floor. A person might think it's safe to run outside for a minute and leave the door unlocked, but that's just the very time, the very second, a maniac will sneak in your house and hide out in the basement.

I can climb over the back fence.

The back door won't open, there's too much snow.

Maybe I can dig a tunnel through.

Sit down while the kettle boils.

No, no, I'm fine, really.

How many times have I told you to leave a spare key with me? I've never known a person to lock themselves out of their own home so often.

Do you have any coffee?

Put these on your feet. I use them for polishing the floor. I put down a coat of wax and then I put these on and I skate all over the floor. So much for my hair lasting the week. Now I've got hat head. Oh, ha ha. The life you have. Your picture was all over the paper yesterday. That's why I was calling you.

I was out.

I was also going to remind you to get a spare key over to me. It's too late now. That's what happens when some people won't answer the phone. I guess now that you're going to be a big star in Toronto you don't have time for anyone from around here.

I'm not going to Toronto.

The newspaper said this big company in Toronto was bringing you up to do your new play.

They changed their minds.

Why?

They had some cutbacks.

They're not going to do your new play?

They still might do it. If they can find a Name.

What kind of a name? A name for the play? Doesn't it already have a name?

No, a Name to *do* the play. They still might produce it, but they don't want me to be in it. They need a Name.

As if you're not a Name.

I'm not famous enough.

Who is more famous than you? Everyone knows who you are. I'm always telling people how famous you are. I'm always telling people that they'll never guess who lives next door to me. They never do guess. I always have to tell them. But, as soon as I tell them, it never fails, as soon as I explain who you are, they are always impressed.

They need a Name. They said if I can find a Name to be in it, they still might do it.

But, if they let you do it, then you'll become a Name.

I don't know any Names. The only Names I know are no better Names than I am. Oh, be some other Name.

Is that from your play?

No, that's from some other play.

Maybe if that was in your play they'd like it so much they wouldn't care if you were famous or not. Have you seen William's picture?

Yes. I've seen it.

That coffin cost ten thousand dollars.

I know.

Maybe if you wrote about that.

About what?

About me and William.
Is there anything to go in this coffee?
Like what? Cream?
No, something stronger.

Part Three

Sometimes I can look at a person's face and see how close they are to being beautiful. Always apply foundation to the face with the tips of the fingers, the very tips only, and always sweep it up and out. Up and out. Up and out. Up and out.

The table is spectacular. The flowers are gorgeous. The place settings are flawless. The makeup looks good enough to eat. Dishes of pink and beige foundations, little cups of sparkling eye shadow, lip cutlery. Everyone is wearing pink. A pink car lounges in the driveway.

"She was practically *purple,* and when you consider that she was wearing blue and green at the time, she looked like a giant *bruise.*"

"Wouldn't it be funny if you wrote a play about my life story? Wouldn't it be funny if you wrote about tonight and all of us were in it?"

"Oh, Et, she doesn't want to write about you. If she won't write about me she won't write about you."

"She might, Bridey."

Mary Kay is expensive. It costs over thirty dollars for one blusher and that doesn't include a brush. The women look at me. I look at the two bottles of wine and calculate. I resign myself to doing penance.

Garbage is strewn all over the street. The garbage men won't take bags filled with glass bottles. Sweep the foundation up. And out. Up. And out. Never apply the makeup in a downward motion. It pulls the skin down like baggy underwear. Up. And out. Light light light.

LOOK AT HER **23**

There's another drinker in the group. Grete. She's got her eye on the Christmas Scotch. "The makeup is the right colour, it's your skin that's off." I'd kill for a smoke. I listen to the women.

"Every time I'm in Toronto I see a play. I see *Phantom*. Every. Single. Time. I love *Phantom*."

The eyeliner is gummy. Mix it with a spit. Here's spit in your eye.

"Et, they took *Phantom* off."

"Of course, that's what I'm saying. Now that they took *Phantom* off, there's nothing to see. There was only that and *Mamma Mia*. Thank God I've got it on the DVD. I don't have to go to Toronto at all."

I can't describe my own work.

"Well, if you can't describe it and you wrote it, maybe they want someone to do it who *can* understand it."

The secret to applying blusher is to suck in the cheeks first. Contour under the jawline disguises a double chin. They look at me as I paint on a new face. I listen. Wouldn't it be funny if I wrote it all down, they ask?

Offensive to Some

Part One

Anyway. How come I'm writin this down is: I wants to make it clear, it wasn't always my dream or nothin to get three months pregnant and go on *Maury Povich* wearin spandex pants. So. Don't go judgin my character or nothin, just cause I was on TV with Maury. They fucken lied. They went and told me I was gonna be the main feature. Then I finds meself squat in between Lorena Bobbitt and Amy Fisher and some chick named Bambi.

Some fun, huh Thumper?

Could'a been worse, I s'pose. Could'a been The *Brady Bunch* reunion. Buncha cunts. Not the *Brady Bunch*. I likes them. It's that *Maury Povich* crowd rots me. Maury didn't like it when I called him Thumper, but I could tell, bein surrounded by all us dangerous women really turned him on. Gave him a real hard-on.

Naw. *Dr. Phil* is the talk show of *my* dreams. He'll do right by me. He really cares about his guests. You can tell by the way he passes out tissues so folks can blow their noses while the commercials is on. Who wants to be on TV with a snotty nose? Yup. It's gonna be a real dream come true for me. I has lotsa dreams. Dreams comes true. Like, when I was little I dreamed that when I grew up I was gonna get married to a really really handsome guy and have three kids and live in a house with a automatic dishwasher and everything like that into it, right? And I did. Then later on I dreamed about killin someone. And I did. So. I knows all about makin dreams come true. That's why I'm writin down my life story. It's kind of, what you calls, inspirational. I wants people to know, no matter what your dream is, you can do it. I wants to be inspirin.

When I'm on with Dr. Phil I'll get to say hi to my kids. They're probably watchin me on TV all the time, now that I'm famous and everything. Greg is four and Wally is seven and Freddy is almost a year. I been practisin. Hi kids. That's what I'll say. Hi. Hi.

The kids is in the attic.

I knows I looks like a piece a shit. I was thinkin, maybe I'll get Dr. Phil's wife, Robin, I can get her to give me one of them-there, what you calls, makeovers. I knows I'm not no beauty queen and I'm not braggin or nothin, but I looked OK when I was pregnant. Jesus. I was hot stuff when I was pregnant. That's the only time in my life I had a figure. I was all juicy and rosy, all ripe like a berry ready to bust. I was, what you calls, orgasmic. I was a big old walkin talkin vagina, permanently pitched on a orgasm. You knows when you're just about to, like, come? You're right there on the brink, right, and you're afraid to even think cause you knows you could lose it but if you could just hang on you could get there, right? Anyway. That was me when I was knocked up. I was a mindless excited little clit. It didn't matter none that I'm not pretty. Nobody looked at my face. All folks saw was my big old achin ripe belly.

Folks can look at my face all they wants to now. They can take a picture. It'll last longer. Pretty soon, I'm gonna be hot stuff again. I'll get my picture on the cover of my book.

You know what the worst thing about bein pregnant is? After you haves your new baby, you got to take it home with you. I'm only joken. Kids is hard work. Like, one time, I'm sittin down foldin up laundry and supper is burnin on the stove and Wally is howlin his guts out and Greg comes over and throws up three bowls of Fruit Loops all over my nice clean folded-up laundry. I thought, you know, I'm never gonna drive through Paris in a sports car with the warm wind in my hair. What the fuck, right? I always got my dreams. Dreams comes true. I dreamed about gettin me some spandex and I got me some spandex. It says on that-there home shopping channel, "Spandex hides a multitude of sins." And I'm a multitude.

The turtle ate the werewolf.

The thing about me is, I knows my rights. I knew all about getting my one phone call. I seen it on *Law & Order*. If it wasn't for TV I wouldn't know nothin. I told 'em right away, right after they arrested me: I needs my one phone call. I think I left the oven on.

Part Two

It runs in the family. There's a whole string of us women, all through the years, we got a really bad strain in us. The first one we knows of lived in eighteen thirty somethin or other. Sylvie, her name was. She lived in Port de Grave too, if you wants to call that livin, livin on the bay in that stink of salt fish and smoke. I should know, I grew up there too, right? So. Sylvie, she's fourteen and her husband's sixty. His first wife died havin, like, their thirteenth kid or somethin, so he went and got Sylvie. Men did that then, right? Men could have two or three wives cause wives was always dyin from havin too many youngsters. So. This old geezer, he wants Sylvie because she's right cute and she's right young and she got this long pretty hair. But then once he gets her, he won't let her do nothin. He won't let her play on the rocks or run through the foam on the beach. "It's not fittin", he says. He won't let her go out with her friends. It's not fittin. He won't let her wear no nice dresses and he won't let her braid no red ribbons into her long hair and she loves her red ribbons. It's not fittin. It's fittin for him to climb on top of her every night and stick his thing into her and her crying and holdin on to her dolly until it's over. Then one night she goes and clocks him over the head with a big old jeezly pipe iron. Now that was fittin. She pitched his body right over the wharf. Gave him to the sea.

I knows all that cause I learned it from the best. That's all Mudder gets on with sometimes. "Be good or ye'll end up like Sylvie! Be good or Sylvie will come and strangle ye with her noose!"

Oh yeah, Sylvie got hanged, right? They went and took her into St. John's and sentenced her to hang from the neck till she was dead. Sylvie fucked em all up though. Turns out she was pregnant. So. They lets her have the baby before they strings her up. Big hairy deal, right? They keeps her locked up for the whole nine months into this big grey stone prison in St. John's. The only company she got is her dolly and her red ribbons. She spends all of her days braidin those red ribbons into her hair. Over and over. Finally she haves the youngster. A girl. One hour after she haves the baby, in they comes to get her. "Time Sylvie! It's time! Say goodbye to that youngster!" So Sylvie, she picks up her daughter and she puts this blessin onto her, and then she puts this curse onto her. Into one ear she whispers, "Listen to your heart." And then into the other ear she says, "But don't go doin what it tells you to do or you're fucked." Nobody knows which one was the blessin and which one was the curse.

Then they marches her off to the gallows. She's cripplin along because the afterbirth is still runnin right out of her, right? There's this priest waitin for her at the very top of the steps. He says, "Does ye repent, Sylvie? Does ye repent afore ye goes to burn for all eternity into the steaming scalding flames of hell?" There's a crowd gathered around and they're all lookin up at the gallows, waitin and waitin to hear what that young girl got to say for herself. She got them red ribbons streamin down her back and red blood is streamin down her legs. And the priest says, "Ask for God's mercy child, on ye and yeres, repent afore ye swings." So Sylvie, she draws herself up right proud and she smiles right sweet-like and she says, "Kiss me arse." She had a noose around her neck but she had them red ribbons in her hair.

I always wanted a daughter. I was some disappointed when I had the boys. It's a queer thing too, nobody says whatever happened to Sylvie's daughter. I likes to walk on the beach and dream about Sylvie. I'm like her. Born in me own grave. Port de Grave. Our beaches is not nice though, not like you sees on TV and stuff, on that-there *Baywatch* with sand and fucken lifeguards bouncing around. Our beaches is full of kelp Jesus that stuff stinks — and dried up old jellyfish and stuff. Still, I can't wait to get back on the beach. That's the first thing I'm gonna do when I blows this pop stand. I got this game I likes. Jump the waves. That's the first thing I'm gonna do. Fuck this for a game of cowboys.

David, that's my husband, David, he's not no ugly old geezer or nothing, not like Sylvie's old man. David's really really handsome. He's dead too. Sylvie had the right idea, givin her old man to the sea. I would'a give my old man to the sea too only the sea would've spit him right back out.

Dead stuff washes out of the sea all the time. Man. There's strange stuff under the water. That's how come I don't know how to swim, right? I'm not goin swimmin around with no dead stuff. There's weird things in there, I'm tellin you. Like, one time, this giant turtle washes up on our beach. It's dead, right? It got a big bite taken out of its guts. It must'a weighed, like, three hundred pounds. I cried, right? I fucken bawled like a baby when I seen that big old dead turtle. Cause. There's stuff in the water we don't know nothin about. Secret stuff. Pretty stuff. Dead stuff. Dead pretty stuff. I loves pretty stuff cause I'm not pretty meself. Mother says, "Ye're a hard lookin old skeet, ye are."

I'm not no slut, though.

When David seen me wearin my brand new spandex pants, he goes, "Only sluts goes around dressed like that." That old slut in me was always poppin out and I'd stuff it back down and it would pop out again and I'd stuff it back down and stuff it back down and stuff it stuff it stuff it. It's like I told Oprah when I was on with her. That's how come I am the inspiration I am today. I let out my inner slut.

I'm after learnin so much from Oprah. That's how come me and her got on so good. I knows her all to pieces. I seen how she lost all that weight. That's how come I'm educated so good, right? I watches TV. I'm what you calls self-edu-cated, right? I wanted to go back to school and get my Grade 10 but David says no good wife should be out goin around where men can look at her and stuff. I'm not allowed to do no home courses either. Jesus, the kids is smarter at books than me. So I says, frig that. I watches *Oprah* and *Maury* and *Dr. Phil*, and *Regis and Kelly* (don't *she* get on my nerves) and I watches *Montel*, and *Jerry*, and *Tyra*. They talks about everythin. TV is way better than books. I learns from the best. The way I figures it is, watchin *Maury* and *Montel* and *Tyra* and that crowd is like goin to high school, and watchin *Oprah* and *Dr. Phil* is like goin to college. I'm some good student too. I watches TV every day from nine to three.

David never found out.

Yeah, I seen how she lost all that weight. She never gave me one of them-there makeovers though. I'd love to look nice now that I'm famous. Anyway, I goes and drops five pounds just to go on the TV and then Alma goes and tells me the camera adds fifteen pounds. Frig.

Alma's in the cell next to me. She's pretty but she don't like nobody lookin at her. Alma says skinny people should be shot. She should know, she's after shootin up a whole bunch of people, but she never killed nobody or nothin, so she's not famous like me. She got it easy. She's one of them-there what you calls paranoid schizophrenics. Fucken mouthful, right? Alma likes to talk, but the thing is, when Alma talks the fucken furniture talks back to her. Now me, they can't find nothin wrong with me. Man, they're tryin so hard to find somethin wrong with me they're goin cross-eyed with the strain.

They says I killed in cold blood. Yeah. I killed in cold blood. I didn't even work up a sweat.

That big old dead turtle is lyin all big and dead and rotten and smelly and squishy on our beach. I climbs right up on top of his shell. I lies right down across it. The smell don't bother me none. We had a outhouse till I was twelve so that's how come I knows how to breathe through my mouth, right? I'm lyin on top of that turtle. I'm thinkin, how grand to have a big mother-fucken thick shell. People is comin in from miles around to look at that turtle. Did you ever hear tell of a famous turtle? I'm lyin on top of that turtle thinkin, it's friggin excellent to be famous. Waving at folks. Hi. Hi. Hi.

Oh yeah, I'm up on top of that turtle wavin at everybody and Mother is down on the beach screamin at me to get down.

Now I am a turtle. Now I'm famous too. Except the turtle was dead. And Sylvie is dead. What's the point of being famous if you're dead? I'm not dead.   When I seen myself on TV, I thought: I could be dead by now for all they knows.

David is a werewolf. When he gets mad he looks at me like I'm lunch. I locks the kids into the attic but I don't got none of them-there silver bullets. A werewolf bit him when he was a kid and that's how come he turned out to be one too. I puts the kids in the attic.

Be right good now. Be right good, like quiet little turtles, OK?

Cause David says, "Make them youngsters shut up or I'll fucken kill em."

He hates me. He hates me when I'm on my period. He thinks I has a period on purpose just so he can't have sex. No, he won't come near me when I'm on my period. He finds it offensive. It's offensive to some. You can pound in my face till you drives my teeth right through my lips. You can stub out your cigars onto my nipples. But God forbid you got to stick your thing into me when I'm on my period.

My period is over now. He starts howlin and I'm the moon. He's takin what he wants and he don't ask. He's sproutin hair and growin fangs and the kids is in the attic. But I'm not.

I don't feel nothin. I got a big thick shell on me.

Then we takes the kids out for ice cream.

One time he peeled off three of my fingernails cause I was wearin red nail polish. Only sluts goes around doin stuff like that. It's like I told Tyra. Fingernails grows back. I never showed Tyra my nipples, though. Probably I might show my nipples on *Jerry Springer*. I could get skin grafts.

I knows, I seen it on *E.R.* But I don't want none. What do a big old turtle want with skin grafts?

Sometimes I'm my own worst enemy.

When I was born, I couldn't hold down milk, right? Mother would feed me and my stomach and bowels would swell right up and I'd go into fits and throw up all over the place. They gets this nurse to come in and she says I'm allergic to cow's milk, right? She says, "Don't give that infant no more cow's milk" So, Fadder says, "Go on. That youngster is pure obstinate, that's all is wrong with her. She was born solid stubborn." Fadder says, "We got no money for goin out gettin special milk. If she gets special treatment now, that's all she's gonna expect her whole life." So, cow's milk is what I got. It didn't matter how sick it made me, right? And I swear to God, by the time I was a year old I could hold it down. Did you ever hear tell of a child who could be so good as that? Mudder and Fadder was some proud of me too.

Mudder and Fadder done what they knew how to do. They reared up me and my eight brothers and sisters. We all got a big filthy mouth on us too. When you got eleven people into the one house you got to figure out some way to get your voice up above the crowd. Our house was always fulla cursin and swearin and laughin and shoutin and jokin and lotsa, you know, lotsa huggin and lovin and stuff. None of us kids never had to go in no attic.

Part Three

Alma is after me to quit smokin. Oh, yeah. They lets me smoke in here. What am I gonna quit smokin for? I got to have somethin to do. I don't drink. I don't do no drugs. I got no bad habits. Not countin murder.

I quit smokin when I had the kids, then I took it up again, then I quit again, then I took it up again, then I quit again, then I took it up again. I'm not quittin no more.

Before I had the kids, all I did was stay in the house and smoke. David was out workin and he said a good wife stays home. So I did. But there was nothin for me to do all day except smoke. The only time I went out was to go buy smokes. One time I went out to buy a pack of smokes and I bought a can of two thousand flushes and took it home and put it in the toilet and flushed it and flushed it and flushed it. Just to see. You know. If you got your money's worth. I thought it was friggin hysterical, right? I wish you could grow your own smokes. I'd like to have a big lawn made out of cigarettes, just growin up out of the ground. Then you want to know what I'd do? I'd go out and light the whole lawn on fire and lie down in the middle of it and I'd smoke. Me, lyin in a big lawn fulla lit-up smokes.

I goes to the doctor one time, right? I tells him I thinks there's somethin wrong with me cause I only goes out of the house to get smokes. And he tells me to quit smokin. I says, My son, you're friggin nuts. If I quits smokin I'll never get outta the house at all. Then he tells me to get pregnant. So I did.

I got a really bad strain in me. Just like Sylvie. The kids knew it from the minute they was born.

What's the point of bein famous if you're dead? Born in me own grave, that's me.

I got a mark onto the back of my neck where he choked me with the phone cord. I got a mark on my chest where he broke my collarbone. I got these nipples. But I still got dreams.

The first few times he hits me, I'm thinkin, this is some kind of mistake. Like I accidentally wandered into somebody else's life. I loves him and he loves me. We loves goin out to movies and to the Ponderosa and stuff. But then it starts. He's goin, "This guy was lookin at you! That guy was lookin at you! I can't take you out nowhere dressed like that! What are you lookin for, you bitch!" Whap. I'm thinkin, look what you're doin, honey. You're makin it too hard for me to forgive you. How come you're makin it so hard for me to believe you when you says you're sorry? And he says he's sorry and give me one more chance and one more chance and one more chance and one more one more one more chance. I gave him so many one-more-chances I used up all my own chances of ever gettin away.

I can wear red nail polish now if I wants to. I can deck myself out in red ribbons if I wants to. I got everybody fucked up. They can keep me locked up in here but they can't stop this baby from growin inside of me.

It's like I told Oprah. I found out there's life after death. He's dead. Now I gets to have my life.

Part Four

They put all that-there yellow tape all over my house. "Crime scene" marked all over the place. My house was a friggin crime scene for years. Where was all their fucken yellow tape then? I calls the cops one time, right? They goes, "No problem here b'ys. Looks like we got a little domestic situation on the go here." A friggin domestic house pet, that's me. I shoulda killed myself then. But it's a sin, right? If you kills yourself then God comes down and stamps "crime scene" on your soul.

Fadder must be spinnin in his grave now. He never wanted me gettin no special treatment. I guess I gets it now. Gets three meals a day brought right in to me. Gets me laundry done. I haves a glass of milk every day.

I guess my brothers and sisters hates me now. They warned me, right? They told me David was too good for the likes of me. He had an education, right? He had his Grade 12. They told me I wouldn't fit in, into the city. In Port de Grave we had a outhouse till I was twelve, but even when we got our nice new bathroom, Mudder still wouldn't let us use it for to do our business in. She said she didn't want nothin stinkin up her nice new bathroom. The bathroom was just for company. So when me and David got married and he took me into the city, I was some excited about our new house. It had one-and-a-half bathrooms into it. But, I couldn't use the toilet. There was no sound of wind nor rain, no one bangin on the door telling me to hurry up. There was no noise to cover up the sound of me doin my pee. I couldn't do my pee cause it was too quiet. See? I didn't even fit into my own house.

David used to come in to Port de Grave to put the Coke in the Coke machines. He had his own truckin business. Me and him would be on the beach playing "jump the waves."

He told me I should always get lots of special attention.

The turtle ate the werewolf. I still loves him, though.

I've got a bit of mornin sickness on the go. I wants all my fans to know I'm doin really great. I'm gettin help and stuff. They're just keepin me locked up cause I've got a really bad strain in me.

I misses the kids. I loved them some lot when they was inside of me. They couldn't see out. Little blind turtles in their shell. It was hard to love them after they was born cause they was always lookin at me. They was always lookin at me when I had a black eye or when me nose was broke or when I had blood runnin down my legs. They was always lookin at me like I was the one doin somethin wrong. They can love me way better now cause they don't have to look at me no more. They can dream of a mudder who's pretty. They can dream a mudder who's not like me. This little turtle I got inside me now, this little one who's makin me so sick, I got a dream for this one. Dreams comes true. This time I'm havin a girl, right? I swear, I has to pee a hundred times a day now. That's life when you're knocked up. I wish somebody would wander into my life, and I could have theirs.

Me and him had magic. David. We'd be on the beach and he'd say, "If the waves touches your toes three times in a row I'll give you a kiss." I told him that I dreamed about gettin married to a really really handsome guy and havin three kids and livin in a house with lotsa lovin and huggin and jokin and stuff into it. And he said, "Dreams comes true."

Part Five

When it all turned right bad, I tried to run away. I showed up on Mudder's doorstep with the kids a hundred times. She'd go and pick up the phone and call him cause she said it was right cruel for us to be makin him worry like that. Then I gave up runnin away because no matter where I went he'd be there waitin for me. He knew I was a turtle. I wasn't gonna get very far with three kids on my back.

Then one time he says, "Next time you runs away I'm gonna have to kill your Mudder."

He says he loves me, though. He says he gets mad cause he loves me so much. He says he broke my nose cause I can't do nothin right. He says that time he held the hot iron on my leg, he says that never happened. He says he stabbed me with the fork because he had a really bad day at work. He says I'm, what-you-calls, paranoid. But he says he loves me. He says I'm his life. He says I'm his life and I'm thinkin, I can't be your life no more, honey. It's killin me.

I'm after givin him a million one-more-chances. How come I don't even get one?

I loves the soaps. I loves the bad girls on the soaps. I thinks it's too bad they never lets the bad girls off with nothin on that TV. They gets to be bad and have a good time for a while, but then they got to fall off a cliff and go into a coma. Bad girls got to die. Then they shows up on commercials sellin toilet paper or on that-there psychic network. I thinks that's a sin. I keeps waitin and waitin for one bad girl to get everything she wants. I wants to be inspirin to bad girls everywhere.

Part Six

A couple of yards out into the water, off the beach in Port de Grave, is this rock. It's my rock. I puts my red ribbons right long into my hair now. They're so long they drags along behind me on the ground. Now they're floatin on the water behind me. They looks like blood. They looks like period blood, right dark. This is my gallows. The water's some deep out here. Lift your arms up. Feel that? That wind is some strong, it could drag me right off and I don't know how to swim, right, so all I got to do is let the wind haul me into the water and I'll drown and be like one of them secret dead things floatin around. Don't go thinkin I wasn't in my right mind. I was in my best mind. I killed him and I wants a bit of glory. You know, it's a queer thing, nobody knows what happened to Sylvie's daughter. I thinks it's me.

That priest fucken lied to Sylvie. She never went to hell. We're all Catholics, right? All you got to do is buy a bunch of them five-dollar masses and you gets into heaven on one of them-there technicalities. Kinda like you got your cover charge paid.

I knows I'm just a walkin talkin crime scene. Still, I wouldn't mind gettin in on a makeover. I put the kids in the attic cause I couldn't save them from the werewolf, but I saved them from turnin out like the werewolf. I had three boys, right? Yeah. Dreams comes true. Even nightmares.

They gets Alma, right, at the friggin grocery store. See, those little voices was talkin to her from inside the fridge tellin her to go shoot the crowd that's supposed to be clearin the snow off the roads. So she did. It's lucky for them that Alma ain't a very good shot. Then on the way home she stops off to pick up a few groceries. They arrested her at the meat counter. And get this, the whole time she isn't wearin nothin but a pair of pantyhose. Not a friggin stitch.

Took five cops to bring me in. There was so much blood on me they thought someone must'a stabbed me a million times. They didn't understand that they shouldn't go fuckin around with someone born in her own grave. I'm walkin down the road, covered in blood, watchin the cars whizzin by and lookin at the trees and the birds and stuff. I had to walk the 800 miles till I got to Port de Grave. I felt right good till the cops come along. They slaps all them chains and cuffs on me. They had no friggin manners, right? I says to em, I says, there's no problem here, b'ys. Just a little domestic situation on the go here.

Part Seven

He's lyin in bed.

He looks some nice when he's sleepin. The kids is makin too much noise. It's not fittin. A pipe iron is too good for the likes of him. There is a knife in my hand.

I can't be your life no more now, honey. It's killin me.

They told me there was blood all over the house, all over the walls, all over the stairs. They told me there was a pile of bones and stuff in the middle of the livin room floor. I hope they don't expect me to clean all that up.

They told me there was blood all over my face and all in my mouth. So much blood and not one drop of it was mine. I can't tell you what a nice change that was. Red ribbons of blood all over the house and not one drop of it mine.

I always liked the view from my rock. I'm the only turtle don't know how to swim, but I'm the only turtle got big sharp teeth. Took the guts right out of that werewolf. Must be all the fucken cow's milk.

My stomach's pookin out already. Little blind turtle in her shell. It's right quiet in there. It's right safe in there too. That's the best place for her to stay. A turtle could have lots and lots of little blind turtles but none of them might survive. I knows, I seen it on TV. I seen it on that *Crocodile Hunter* show before he died. Cause, you know, stuff happens to them. Stuff happens. Sylvie. She went and had her youngster, her girl. Now that was pure selfish. Sendin that child out into the world with this really bad strain into her. Sendin me out with this really bad strain in me.

I'm not fucken sayin I'm sorry to nobody. I done what I knew how to do and I learned from the best. So that's how come I'm writing this down for what-you-calls posterity.

Kiss me arse.

The Widow's Walk

(Widow's Walk: A small railed observation platform atop a house, overlooking the sea. Also known as a Belvedere. An architectural distinction. A woman's place to wait and watch.)

There isn't enough room in the harbour to hold all the ships. The water is tortured with the schooners, the Two-Masted, the Square Topsails, the Three-Masted, the Four-Masted, the Generals, the Grand Bankers, the Terns. The bay is forested with masts. Anyone who pleases can walk on the water, cross the bay by stepping from deck to deck. The big flat-arsed manly boats rub up against each other, chafing from being named after women.

The men sail out and the women wait. They know who the other woman is. They know what she is.

A girl sits at home, sewing on her wedding dress. Not a fancy dress. A plain dress meant to be worn after the nuptials. She is stitching the hem when she feels a chilling draft sweep through the room. There is no window open. The fire burns in the wood stove, but the heat of it can no longer be felt. She looks around and shivers. She tries to stand up but sits again from the puzzlement of feeling water drizzle on her shoulder. She feels a rough hand touch her on the back of her neck, and she hears the voice of her sweetheart. "My maid. Leave the dress now. I only come for to say goodbye." She faints.

She comes to, the room again toasty, the fire crackling. There is no one else with her. There is only the damp imprint of his hand on the back of her shoulder, and salt water all over the floor. She does not pause. She sets back to work straight away, taking apart the wedding frock. She begins a new one, made all of black. She finishes it in one night and puts it on. She climbs to the Widow's Walk, a widow without ever being married, and waits for the schooner that will never be seen again.

She's waiting still.

Woman in a Monkey Cage

Part One

I'm dying for a smoke, and a shot of Scotch, one of those cheap Scotches that burns all the way down and chews the insides out of you. I'll have a shot glass filled with Scotch please, brimming over with it. Start pouring and forget to stop. I'll lick it up off the floor and off the side of the glass and drink it down so goddamn fast it starts a fire in my guts. I'll pour Scotch all over my arms and legs and lips and then light up a cigarette. The Scotch will kiss me and I'll kiss the cigarette and go up in flames.

There is no avoiding the future once you know what's going to happen.

The new cage is fine. It's bigger. I can see some of the others from here. I can see the snot-faced little monkey. It's too bad about the elephant. No more elephants. But that just goes to show you. Survival is everything. I don't mind they moved the monkey into the elephant's cage.

But they could have changed the sign on mine.

There is no sense in crying. It must have been the stress that finally got to it. I'm used to stress. I'm a hairstylist. Beauty is a very stressful business. I've got women coming in; they don't need a new hairstyle. They need a frigging miracle. They need a shrink. They come in looking for a new haircut when what they really want is a new life. They come in looking for a new life so I give them a perm and a colour and a fruit-acid face peel. A fruit-acid face peel isn't easy; you can burn the face off someone.

It's up walking around like that which is not natural. It's dead. I watched it die. The dead should go lie down somewhere. My fingers hurt.

I miss being touched. I miss sex. I tried to tell them about sex but I don't know if they understand me. Sex is like riding a bike. Same thing. Women can go for bike rides and think about anything at all. Men are very bike obsessed. Women go for long bike rides. Men go for shorter bike rides. If you fall off the bike you get pregnant. I've got a ten-speed between my legs.

I've got a name. My feelings are very hurt about that monkey sign.

A place for everything and everything in its place. Woman's in the monkey cage and all is right with the universe. It doesn't matter because I'm safe. I'm safe in my place because I know where my place is. I'm safe, we're all safe, no need to get hurt. I'm safe, we're all safe, no need to get hurt.

I know what they want.

I know what I want. I'd like a mirror. I can't remember what I look like. I close my eyes and try to picture my face but all I see is Michelle Pfeiffer. She's got good hair. She had good hair.

Everything is alien here. Even me. Especially me. I want to shave all the hair off my body so there won't be anything animal about me. There's hair coming in on my legs and growing in under my arms, and my eyebrows need to be plucked before they grow together. I want to scrape myself bald from head to toe, everywhere. I just want to know I'm not a monkey. I want to be soft and smooth and clean. I want someone to talk to.

I could talk to Joe till I was blue in the face.

Joe? You should have been in the shop today, Joe. Mrs. Rose came in. She was after giving herself a home perm on top of the nice streaks I put in for her. Her hair was fried, Joe. She looked like a poodle, Joe. As a matter of fact, Joe, she turned into a fucking poodle, right there in the shop, Joe, all yipping and yapping, and I took her to the pound, Joe.

Joe, he just sits and reads the paper and nods his head. And there's me, right in the middle of saying something really important, and he says, "What's for supper?" And there's me standing there with all my feelings hanging down around my ankles. It sure did make my fingers hurt. Don't get me wrong, we had a good marriage. The only reason we got divorced is he moved away.

Me and Amelia Earhart. Me and her, same thing. I flew away and never came back. She made the world smaller. She shrank the ocean to the size of a headline. "First Woman to Solo Across the Atlantic." I stole the newspaper clipping out of the library. I took all the miles and miles of ocean and folded them up and put them in my pocket. People are still looking for me, but Amelia Earhart's never coming home.

I took flying lessons once. This old guy had a bush plane, him and the plane both pretty racked up. This old guy, Cyril, takes my money up front and then he tells me there are no refunds. No-where-no-way-no-how. He looks at my chest. He's looking at my chest like, you know, get a load of them. I button up my coat and he starts to sulk and then I feel bad. So I open up my coat again and give him what he wants. I figured it was worth the flash if it saved me some cash. Guess again. No fucking discount. He loves his plane too much. Loves it, strokes it, pets it, calls it honey, baby, sweetie, love. Cyril. He's all mixed up. He treats women like planes and planes like women.

Cyril crashed in his plane. His honey took him face and eyes into the side of the Torngat Mountains. Smacked him upside a cliff. Love is blind. He got burned up in flames. So, Cyril was right. Getting a refund was definitely out of the question. His plane wasn't the woman, though. I was the woman. Me and Amelia are dying for a smoke. I could eat a cigarette.

The elephant didn't give them what they want. It never made a sound the whole time it was here. They couldn't record it. The ghost has no voice.

I was born in the zoo with the monkey and the elephant.

Part Two

Oh Great Spirit who flew in on the wind, you haven't used your wings in ages; it's time now to begin. Can't dream on stars, there's things in space, but you can fly to another place. Here is the door, I cut it wide, now use the door.

Now Spirit leave this body to herself and fly. Now spirit leave this body to herself and fly. Now Spirit leave this body to herself and fly and fly and fly.

When I was little, Social Services came to our house and tried to take away my brothers and me. We had gone to school with little cuts all over our fingers. We had the croup. Mom took us to the doctor but she also took a little knife and sliced little nicks all over our hands. She was letting out the bad spirit that was making us sick. Welfare said she was another crazy Indian.

Daddy was a crazy Irishman. He worshipped the ground Mom walked on because she gave him all those sons. She gave him me too. Daddy worshipped me too. Joe was crazy for me too, at first, and I'm telling you, once you've had that kind of love with someone, anything after that is only a faded colour, like a shirt washed out too many times.

Mom told me stories.

"I was walking by the woods one day. A bear ran out of the woods at me. Now, child, watch him in your mind. Here he comes! Watch him, so big, you would not think he could move so fast. He runs like he is in one of my dreams, strong and fast, muscles rippling like a brook over his bones. He is running like a river of water. I raise my rifle, raise your rifle, but wait for the sure shot. The sure shot only comes one time. My pee is hot down my legs but I hold still. The bear is smiling a big old smile so I can see his teeth. He sees my rifle and smells my fear: that is OK, let him know me for what I am. See his eyes. See his yellow teeth. Know him for what he is. Now take your shot. Clean. Right between the eyes. His blood is on me, to mark me with his respect. When I told my good father what had happened, he turned grey with fright. He told all his friends how lucky I was to escape with my life. Then he sold the bear skin. But now, I will tell you, I was not lucky. I was strong. My father was the lucky one. He got a skin for free. I took a new name after that. I took the bear's name. A name is very important."

They will let me out. They don't see me for what I am yet. But they will. And when my blood ends up on them, then they will know my respect.

Part Three

I woke up and it was out there looking in at me. I'm afraid of it. The only thing free to walk around and it's dead. It opens its mouth and no voice comes out. It has no voice. It makes us nervous. The monkey, the lion, me.

I'm dreaming a lot. I dream about earth. I dream about getting out of this cage and walking out into that big grey space. Last night I dreamed I was a monkey. Maybe the monkey has nightmares too. Maybe it dreams it's a woman and wakes up screaming.

The elephant's soul is trapped in that body. I pray it keeps away from me.

I looked up to see the sky turn red with the big ships. Big red balloons hanging in the sky like some giant is having himself a birthday party. Everything was red. Someone was screaming her lungs out. The bad spirit flew out.

I love my keeper. My watcher. I press up against the door. I like to be looked at. One time, one time, I wish the door would open. I need to touch something. We could stand beside each other, side by side, and just barely feel each other. That skin looks like leather. I bet it feels nice and soft like leather.

We could sway next to each other, bend and stretch, and I can bend and stretch too. We can dance.

Not one soul had asked me to dance the whole night. I was spending all my time hiding in the bathroom so no one would know I was a wallflower. I went to the bathroom twelve times in a row. And then the band started to play "Sweet Dreams." And then Joe came over.

I don't know how to dance too good. Like this? Your name is Joe? Hi, Joe. My name is, shit you're stepping on my foot, Joe. You smell good, Joe. You smell like wash just taken in off the line.

I'm safe here. I know. I am not judged. I told them I had a kid. On earth. She was four. I can't say her name out loud. If I say her name out loud, I'll go nuts. I was a good mom. Sometimes after the divorce, you know, I'd be too tired to cook, so I'd give her Cheerios for supper. But I was a good mom. She had dark eyes. Elephant eyes.

I haven't had a period since I got here. And I'm not eating anything. They try to feed me bananas when I'm sleeping. I don't need to eat and I don't need my period. When I got my first period I called up my best friend and told her I broke something inside me from jumping off the bed too hard. She laughed to kill herself. She told me I didn't have to go to gym cause I was on the rag. I got to hang out behind the school and smoke with all the other ones. I joined the secret club. I wanted to send out announcements. I wanted to walk up to strangers on the street and say, "I got my period!" It doesn't take long, though, until you figure out what the real deal is. The real deal is you get told by the school nurse that it's a wonderful gift, then you find out it's called The Curse. Mom got me the big blue Kotex box. The big long pads with the strips on each end to hook and tie. Waddling around with the big canoe strapped between your legs. Hoping no boys would notice. Hoping everyone else would. Hoping they would notice a real woman waddling among them. Since my periods stopped I've got no way of keeping track of time.

Their silence is starving me. I wonder if the elephant was female, if it had any kids. Maybe that's what happened to it. It said its child's name out loud and it went insane. Maybe that's what happened. There are things to do to stop thinking about the bad stuff. I count in my head.

I had a dream. In my dream you talked to me. You told me that when I gave you everything you wanted you would let me out. Or you would kill me.

Part Four

Now Spirit leave this body to herself and fly. Now Spirit leave this body to herself and fly. Now Spirit leave this body to herself and fly and fly and fly.

I need a razor blade.

I've got a half-moon scar in between my toes. I was four. I was jumping off the pump house with garbage bags tied to me. I was planning to fly but I had a crash landing on a piece of glass. I half hoped my big toe was going to come off. I've got a little bone that sticks out funny on my ankle. I was eight. I was dancing in the Christmas concert with Jerome Hickey. We were stepping away and he kicked me hard in the ankle. I was hopping around so much everyone thought I made up some new kind of step. We got a standing ovation. After the concert I kicked him back. Then I gave him a standing ovation and asked him how he liked it. I've got a burn scar on the back of my knee. I got too close to the bonfire on my first drunk. I was thirteen. I climbed out of my bedroom window and sneaked off to the Protestant graveyard. That's where we did our drinking, with the dead Protestants. The drunk Catholics and the dead Protestants, all the sinners in the one spot. If you're dead you should go lie down somewhere. Fucking elephant. I've got stretch marks. I've got a little lump in my right ear. I tried to pierce my ears with ice cubes and a darning needle. I got that needle halfway through my ear before I passed out. I hit the floor cold junk. My life story is written all over my body. Read me like Braille. All the little scars on my fingers are from the times I felt bad and I had to let out the bad spirit. When I feel bad my fingers get to paining out loud. I count the scars to pass the time.

Part Five

Being saved from certain death and put in an intergalactic zoo is the very best thing that ever happened to me. I am saner now than I ever was. I wish I had some lipstick. I would do a monkey makeover.

They've gone. They've been gone a long time. My watchers. They are not playing by the rules. Fucking ugly looking keepers. I'm talking; I'm talking so they're supposed to be here. I'm hot. My fingers are on fire. I'll write them a story so hot they'll have to spit on it to read it. I'm talking.

I like to look pretty. It's a flaw. I never gave up trying. I did it all. I had sixteen different shades of lipstick and shoes and purses to match. When I went to the bank to get a loan, to open up my own beauty salon, the manager tells me I can't get a loan unless my husband co-signs it with me. So I march in to that bank, I'm not telling a word of a lie, and I look that three piece, stuffy arsed suit right in the tie. "I've been working since I was fifteen. My little bank account here doesn't mean much to you, but right after I close it I'm getting my best friend Carla to close hers. Then I'm getting all the girls at the Wash & Spin to close theirs. Then I'm getting Marla to close hers and she sells Mary Kay and drives a pink Mercedes." Yeah. I did that. I got the loan. And I know, I know in my heart of hearts that I had the confidence to go do that because I was wearing Revlon Purple Passion Creamy Fresh Lip Lustre # 2.

I'm a winter. That was my specialty, in the salon, doing colours. So, I know, I'm a winter. I look good in a burgundy or deep red. Hey, got a light? Got a smoke? Got a minute?

Come back. I miss you. Come back.

Part Six

I was out on the water from the time I was a child. I was at it off and on for years. I fished until I got retrained. I fished better than some of the men. The next best thing to flying is sitting on top of the water. When I'm fishing I forget everything. Joe used to torment me. "A woman wanting to fish. I suppose the next thing you'll want to pee standing up." I said, "Who wants to piss in the wind? I'd rather sit down to pee. It's more dignified and it keeps your hands free." Joe laughed. I thought he'd die laughing. Me and Daddy and Joe fished together. The rest of the men were pissed. "She's going to cause trouble. A woman fishing is bad luck." Someone forgot to tell the fish. They were good years. The government wouldn't give me unemployment benefits that first season. They said there was no way that little old me was hauling in so many fish. They said some man must be letting me have his catch. They changed their minds, though. Daddy and Joe dumped a truckload of fish guts on the front steps of the unemployment office. I was pregnant then. I had to quit anyway.

Joe stopped talking when they closed the fishery. He stopped talking and I couldn't shut up. I had to fill in all his gaps with my words. Voices came spilling out to eat up the silence. I got retrained. I had a choice. I could be a home-care worker or a hairstylist. The world is my oyster. Joe wouldn't take retraining. He went to the mainland to work in a factory. We divorced. That's how I ended up in to the city with my own hair salon. It's not as fancy as it sounds. I'd work fourteen hours a day. Go home too tired to stand up straight. Throw some Cheerios in a bowl for the little one. Tuck us both in.

The spaceships came, Joe. Honest to God, like in some kind of movie. One minute I'm standing there and the next thing I know I'm floating up. I look down and everything is getting smaller and smaller. I tried to grab her up and take her with me. I tried. Do you blame me, Joe?

Part Seven

The men are upset with me. They think I'm crazy. They think I'm going to stir up trouble because I can hear voices and they can't.

Joan of Arc. For the last time. We implore you. Go before the people and renounce the voices.

It's true.

Renounce the voices and we will let you out of the cage.

No, wait.

Renounce the voices and we will set you free.

I'm telling the truth. It's true. I was there at the movie when it happened. Ingrid Bergman got all her hair cut off. She looked pretty. She didn't look like a boy.

I looked like a boy. When I was little my hair was long. Once I took the scissors and chopped it. I had the itch. The nuns put lye all over my head and burnt the scalp off me, so I went home and finished the job. Daddy tormented the life out of me. "Hey there, young fella." I went around with a stocking cap on my head. I looked like one of my brothers. I bet Ingrid Bergman never had the itch.

They put me on a stake. They're going to burn me alive. My God. My God. Why hast thou forsaken me.

Wait, no, that was Jesus. He heard voices too, only he got nailed to a cross.

They burned me up and I flew and flew and flew. I flew up into the sky and me and Amelia Earhart are never going back.

I've got no hair. I'm a boy, like my brothers. Daddy loves me now because I'm a boy too. We do boy stuff. I like throwing rocks at the Protestants and stealing plums out of trees. I am not afraid that there is someone hiding under my bed. Daddy needs a new deckhand for his boat. John Kelly's boy lost three fingers in a winch and he's got gangrene. Daddy's asked all around the harbour, but it's too late in the season and all the young lads are hired out. One day after supper Daddy winks at me and says "How about it, young fellow?" And I wink back at him. I'm proud.

I'm a boy. I didn't lose my fingers to a winch. I don't have to sit with my knees stuck together. I don't have to be clean all the time. I can piss in a beer mug when no one is looking.

The seagulls follow the boat in a big fluffy cloud, white and pretty and shitting over everything. I hear their voices. They screech out to me, "YOU'RE A BOY!" I call back, "I'M A BOY! I'M A BOY!"

After the summer was over I had to go back to school. I was beaten by the nuns. They didn't see it. They didn't get it.

I'm a boy, Sister. I'm a boy. I'm not wearing a fucking skirt. I am so a boy. I've got a dick. I'm going on the boat with my daddy again next summer and then you'll see. I'm even getting my own stitch.

If you're on a boat you've got to have your own stitch knit into your sweater. In case you fall overboard and drown and the fish eat the face off you. When you wash up on shore, if you do, they can tell who you are by the stitch in your sweater. That's why they call them fishermen's knits.

Mom? I've got a stitch in my chest. It hurts to breathe. There's something wrong with my chest, it's all swelled up into funny bumps. There and there, see? Daddy! Mom's making me wear a bra! Daddy? Yeah. Yeah, I get it. I guess I am a young woman now...

He broke my heart when he told me that. I cried and cried because I couldn't be a boy anymore. I couldn't go back out on the boat. I had to go babysitting for the Kearlys. And I had to watch in underneath my bed.

I renounce the voices. Let me out now.

Part Eight

We are so sorry we could not save your planet from exploding. We did send a warning to your very intelligent cat life forms. You did not listen. You put the cat out. It is beyond our means to correct the terminal atmospheric damage suffered by Earth. We did attempt to help. We have read your most popular worldwide best-selling novel *The Bible* by Mr. Gideon. We see you have had trouble with the world ending before. So we decided to save two of everything. Unfortunately, due to computer error, we were only able to save one of everything. Please forgive this inconvenience. Watcher, the one who watches, will record what you are. This record will be kept forever. Thank you for your co-operation in this matter.

I put the cat out. I thought it was in heat. I took it to the vet and had it fixed.

Part Nine

Remember. When you're rolling your perm the secret is all in the size of the rods and in keeping your ends neatly wrapped. Now when plucking the eyebrow follow the natural arch. Pluck in the direction that the hair is growing. Don't fool with that natural arch or you end up with a woman looking permanently stunned.

Just now I looked out and I thought I saw the water. I wonder if they saved one ocean.

This is how you stand in a boat. You've got to roll with it. Don't fight the swell or your stomach will let you know. You grab onto that net and haul it in until your back is cracking. Hand over fist. That sea is rolling and that net is hauling the skin off your fingers and hauling the pain out of you.

My goddamn nail just cracked off.

Where the fuck do you get off, anyway? I hate your fucking guts Mr. Leather-Tree-Space-Man. You won't talk to me. You won't even talk to me.

I am still sane. I am still sane. I am still sane. I got through the bay and the boys and the booze. I got through the shit. I was OK. I was OK as long as I was out on the water. Till they shut it down.

You'd better never let me out of here. If you do, the first thing I'm going to do is fucking kill you. You ugly leather stupid tree twit fuck. I'm going to take the sure shot and sell your skin.

Part Ten

This is my dream: I'm walking down a long road. It's a dirt road. Scuff your feet. See the dust fly up? The bushes and the trees are reaching out to touch me. I'm tired. I'm hot. I see a big rock. I sit on the rock so I can have a rest.

Get off me.

Who's that? Who's that talking to me? I'm scared.

It's me. It's the rock.

Rocks can't talk.

Well, I am talking to you so I must be able to talk.

How is it you can talk?

I have been here forever. I have been fine. But now you sit on me and that is not fine with me. So I tell you to get off. The only time to make yourself heard is when you have something to say.

Thank you, Rock.

Thank yourself. Now get off me.

So I get off. But the rock won't talk to me anymore. Then I wake up and I'm still in here. Mom told me:

"One time the reverend asked me to write down the story of my life so far. So I did. It took a long time. I do not read or write so good. But he lost it. This does not mean my life is lost. But this means that now I will only give him a little bit of my life. The less I give, the more he will keep. The more I give, the more there is to be lost."

I wanted to be a strong woman like her. She told me all women are strong. They just need to know it's safe to show it.

Here. This is a tear. You can have it. Tears are wasted on me.

Part Eleven

This bird flew too high chasing clouds, wanting to land in them. This bird fell hard before learning about clouds. This bird looks up in an alien sky and glides. This bird flies with a heart of stone. Amelia Earhart's never coming home.

The thing about Amelia Earhart is, she went down in the Pacific somewhere. People kept looking for her, all the time looking for her. They wouldn't give her any peace. I saw a bunch of men on the news holding up her shoes. That's a frigging lie. You don't need shoes to fly.

I love that fucking dead elephant. It just stopped eating. It starved itself to death. I've been watching that elephant. I'm a watcher too. I saw them stuff it and animate it and get it up walking around. I see how it never goes where it is supposed to. I see it come up to the cages and look in at us with its black eyes.

She spoke her child's name to me. I heard her voice. I told her my name.

I dreamed I was on the Earth again and the spaceships came. But this time I grabbed her up in my arms and we floated up here together. I'm not sad. I dreamed the door to this cage opened and I was afraid to walk out. I dreamed I was an elephant. I wonder who will get the monkey cage this time. I wonder if they'll change the sign. I haven't had anything to eat in such a long time. It feels good. My period started again today. It's just flowing right out of me.

When you stuff me and animate me and get me up walking and talking, you'll get my blood all over you. You'll have my respect. I have a name. My name is…

DaddyButt

This is going to be my lucky night. I just know it. Going to the Bingo with DaddyButt is always excellent. It's delightful. But tonight is going to be the best. I can feel it.

DaddyButt's only got one good leg. He's got one good leg and one crippled leg because he got hit by a car once. He has to use a cane. That's too bad because he's only got one good eye. He's got one good eye and one bad eye. I think that's all right because his good eye balances out his bad leg, and his good leg balances out his bad eye.

DaddyButt and me get along very well. We get along because we do not have to talk to each other. We like to sit around together and read books and magazines. If all everyone did was sit around and read together and stop talking all the time the world would be a much better place.

I'm five years old but I don't know how old DaddyButt is. I can read better than anyone else I know except for him. I read *Alfred Hitchcock's Mystery Magazine* all the time. It is terribly hard for people to let you read in peace. We like to read at the dinner table. You put your plate in front of you and prop your book up behind the plate and eat without dropping anything on the pages. But do you think the real world will leave you in peace? It's all "No reading at the dinner table. It's not polite." Reading is more polite than talking, if anyone would ever ask me. Talking leads to arguing and arguing leads to bad feelings and bad feelings lead to broken dishes and the next thing you know someone's crying and being carted off to The Mental, thinking the world is being invaded by spaceships. Reading can also take your mind off the fact that the food is not very good.

When I started school this year I thought there would be many excellent books to read. Books the size of trucks. Instead, Sister gave us a stupid book about a little yellow duck. It only had ten pages in it and most of those are taken up with stupid pictures. The words are all in extra big print, as if words in extra big print will make you a better reader. That is like shouting at a deaf person. I know all about deaf people because DaddyButt has only got one good ear.

I got the strap for reading that book too fast. The only thing that happened in the book was that the little yellow duck swam from one side of a puddle to the other, and then back again, and then back again, and then back again. That book clearly demonstrated a lack of imagination. Not like in *Alfred Hitchcock's Mystery Magazine* where husbands bury wives beneath rose bushes. Another example of what too much talking can lead to.

I hate school. Sister does not want me to read quickly, but Renalda Hickey is being held back because she's slow. Sister told me not to use my big words in class like I think I'm better than anyone else. Then she gave me the strap because I would not get up in front of everyone and talk about what I did on my summer vacation. What is it they want? Talking? Or no talking?

What I did on my summer vacation was read the Bible.

DaddyButt is a writer. He writes plays. He wrote an excellent play. It was very amusing. It was about a man walking around town pushing a baby carriage. He visited all his friends. They looked in the baby carriage and said, "Oh my, how sweet is that. How nice for you to come by! How gorgeous." Then they took a bottle of rum from out of the baby carriage.

DaddyButt is the only person I know who can make the ghosts behave. He and MommyButt lived in an old house once. It was very nice except for the fact that every time DaddyButt went to play cards with the priest all the ghosts came out in the house and tortured MommyButt. That house was always full of ghosts. They would materialize and stomp around and slam the doors. So someone would always have to fetch DaddyButt to come home. And as soon as he came home the ghosts went away. So he could read in peace.

DaddyButt smokes a pipe and I like the smell of it so much I borrow it occasionally. DaddyButt is old and venerable, and so am I. If only everyone would stop treating me like a five-year-old.

DaddyButt does not seem like a grown-up to me. He's more like me. Wise beyond his years. Grown-ups do not make sense. They say a child should be seen and not heard. They tell you to put down that book and get outside and play. How are you supposed to get outside and play if you have to be seen and not heard? No one will play with you if you stand there like a numbnuts. I know. You have to be seen *and* heard. Then you have to come inside for dinner and don't open your mouth to talk back and clean off your plate. How am I supposed to clean off my plate if I can't open my mouth? Clean off that plate because there are starving children in Africa, who are more than welcome to have my dinner if they're so hard up. I don't know why some people bother to have children.

These are the only things I hate about my life so far: not being able to read at the dinner table, going to school and mother being in The Mental. Sister told me I could be in the choir. She told me I could stand in the front row because I'm the correct height, but she also told me not to sing, just to move my lips. Be seen and not heard. Again.

I win quite a lot when I'm at Bingo, but I'm too shy to call out. I win the Four Corners, or the Straight Line, or sometimes the Full Card. I sit there and I sit there trying to work up the courage to call out. Someone else always beats me to it and I have to watch while the money goes into the wrong hands.

One of these days, and I think it will be tonight, I will have the courage to call out when I win. Everyone will look at me and DaddyButt will give me a sip from out of his flask.

I like Bingo because there is no talking, only listening to the man calling out the numbers. All the decisions are made.

I think tonight will be the night when I will get all of the winning numbers. And I will call out. My only worry is that I am shorter than everyone else so I might be heard and not seen.

Confessions of an Aging Ingénue

I've had a good career as an actor. I've worked all over the country and in different parts of the world. Yet, I remain humble. I know I am not as famous as Cathy Jones and I know I never will be.

A woman from City Hall in St. John's called me. She said, "Berni. I'm calling on behalf of the City of St. John's. We're having a very important national conference next year, and we're only having the best of everything. We're having the best in catering. The best in facilities. The best in music. And we wanted the very best comedienne on the East Coast of Canada. But Cathy Jones is busy. So, that's why I'm calling you. Do you have a number for Mary Walsh?"

So, go ahead and hate me because I'm beautiful. Many people ask me: Is all that gorgiosity that's oozing out of you natural, or is it fake? I tell them the truth. It's fake. My face takes work. I've got a face like the Trans-Canada Highway. It's always got a hole in it somewhere. Every morning when I get up I've got to lay down the asphalt. I plaster on the foundation, the powder, the blusher, the concealer, the eye shadow, the eyeliner, the mascara, the eyebrow pencil, the lip pencil, the lipliner, the lipstick, the lip gloss. Then I spray the whole jeezly works of it with Windex. Keeps it all in place. I hate it when you go outdoors and your face blows off. All in all, it takes me roughly five hours a day to achieve my natural beauty. And that's only if I'm going out to get groceries. A big event can take up to three days. If I didn't live in Newfoundland I would not be half as gorgeous as I am today. My kind of beauty stands out better against a backdrop of bleak depression and poverty. I'm not the worst looking woman around. I might have a face on me like a make-work project, but when I look around at the crowd I hang out with I think: infrastructure rehaul.

I'm not one for false modesty. I've got no time for false modesty. I can only hope I live to be 90, because I'm more than halfway there. I went to bed on the night of my 45th birthday and everything was normal. I looked just like Julia Roberts. The next day I woke up and first of all there was a pouch around my middle that wasn't there before, and second of all there was the sudden onset of the underarm wattle. If there's a good gale of wind out I can get airborne. The underarm wattle must be where all our sins are deposited. The bigger your wattle, the more fun you've had.

So now I'm in my 40s but I wasn't done with my 30s yet. I'm getting wrinkles and zits at the same time. I went shopping the other day and I experienced abuse of the elderly for the first time. I went into a store called La Senza. Like Victoria's Secret, only Canadian. I only went into the place because I was looking for a pair of underdrawers. The plain kind that come up to cover your gut and go down enough to cover the top of the wobbly thigh bits. The nice normal kind with the snappy elastic around the middle that cinches in your overhang. Next thing I know this snippy little salesgirl comes bouncing up to me. The zippadee-doo-da-daytype. "Hi, how are you today!" I said, "Frig off, I'm forty frigging five!" You should have heard me what she called me, right to my face. She called me "Ma'am." She was under 30, so she had to die.

This year I lost out on roles because I was either too young, too old, not well enough known, too well known, or I wasn't Cathy Jones. I remember as a child being told that I could be pretty if I tried. So, all these years later, I'm still trying. I'm getting some botulism. That's like salmonella for your face. It's all the rage. It's Botox. It's a poison and they stick it into your face with little needles so it paralyses you and you can't move a muscle. You are left with absolutely no self-expression but that's OK. I don't believe in self- expression.

I try to take care of myself. I make it a point to never drink or smoke anymore … at the same time. I get up and walk at least once a day to the fridge, instead of skooching over on the humpty like I used to. I joined a health club last month because I wanted to lose a few pounds. I still have a bit of baby fat to lose because I had a baby there 24 years ago. I'm the only one I know who's got butt crack coming and going. Anyway, the frigging health club does not frigging work. One hundred bucks a month and I have not lost an ounce. I called them up and told them right off. I told them it was all a big rip-off. They said, "Missus. For the health club to work, you've actually got to show up." I tried exercise and I hate it. I showed up for an aerobics class and I couldn't find an ashtray anywhere. The trainer said that to start out we were going to loosen up and I said, "Great, I'll have a rum & Coke." I had to do jumping-jacks while dumping ashes in the palm of my hand.

So, I'm getting plastic surgery. I'm getting the works, styrofoam implants, collagen and hydrofoam and plasticine. I'm getting my face sandblasted. They can do this thing now where they suck all the fat out of your backside with a big needle and inject it into your lips. I might end up with cellulite on my face but at least no one will have to bend over to kiss my arse.

Anyway, I found out that there are a lot of similarities between aerobics and sex. All that panting and moaning and groaning and sweating. You always look a lot better going in than you do coming out. But at least after aerobics you haven't got to pretend it was the best class you ever had in your life. I quit all the exercise, anyway. It was bad for my health. I accidentally swallowed a cigarette.

I went out and bought the very latest, hottest, fashion torture device known to humankind: the push-up braserette. This is why certain objects on my body appear larger and slightly higher than they actually are in real life. The push-up bra uses the same technology they use on the space shuttle. Anything to defy gravity. It's like strapping a can opener on to the front of your chest. It's made of wire, steel, bone, sutures, labradorite – metric tonnes of pressure fastened around your chest. How it works is, it sucks every available ounce of fat up off your body and shoves it up under your chin. You can be guaranfriggingteed it was never tested out on animals. It cost me $46 plus tax (at La Senza), $46 for an item of clothing to be worn underneath your clothing. Did I mention the underwire? Never mind raising my boobs. You can raise the dead with this thing. Right now parts of me are in a different time zone. When I take off my push-up braserette at night my feet pop right out of my shoes. I like the cleavage. It's where I keep my wallet. There is no equivalent piece of clothing for men. I can't explain the sensation of wearing the push-up braserette, unless a man wanted to go pay $46 to have his dangly bits attached to a forklift. Maybe I could get a grant for that.

The worst thing is there was a matching $56 thong to go with the push-up braserette. Which I bought. I put it on last night before I went to bed, and when I woke up this morning it had disappeared. I may need surgery to take it out. The doctor will wonder what the frig I was doing with the dental floss. Women can buy bras now that come with air bags. They've got little sacks in them, and they come with a little bicycle pump and you blow them up until you get the size you want. I don't know what happens if you get a blowout. And they come with water bags now, filled with water for that natural look. Not very nice when you're outside and it's 20 below. You end up wearing ice cubes in your bra. Talk about shrinkage. I blame it all on Sir Isaac Newton. Him and his frigging law of gravity. If not for him, my breasts would levitate toward my forehead.

Well. Shopping is still good therapy. Retail therapy still beats drugs. Men don't like to go shopping with women. Men don't understand that for us shopping is a religious experience. We're not looking for a new outfit. We're looking for a frigging miracle. Little wonder we need to read books like *Women are from Mars, Men are from Gander*.

Men don't understand women. They don't understand us when we say, I'm getting my hair cut because I'm growing it out. Or when we say, I'm eating this whole entire chocolate cake all by myself tonight because I'm going on a diet tomorrow. Men don't understand why women need to hear *I love you.*

YOU NEVER SAY YOU LOVE ME.

WHAT HAVE I GOT TO SAY IT FOR. I'M HERE, AREN'T I?

YEAH, BUT I LIKE TO HEAR IT.

I SAID IT THAT TIME LAST YEAR.

I LOVE YOU.

ME TOO.

SEE? I KNEW YOU DIDN'T LOVE ME CAUSE YOU NEVER SAY YOU LOVE ME SO YOU DON'T FRIGGING LOVE ME, DO YA, DO YA, DO YA.

ALL RIGHT. ALL RIGHT. ALL RIGHT. I LOVE YA. I LOVE YA. I LOVE YA, LOVE YA, LOVE YA. ALL RIGHT? NOW PASS THE FRIGGING CLICKER.

Sometimes it's hard to be a woman. It's hard to be a good Catholic woman. We're not allowed to use birth control, have premarital sex or get divorced. I have done all three but I'm hoping to slip into heaven. That way when I die I can hang around in the lounge while they get my table ready in heaven. I'll have a few Bloody Marys at the bar until I get to break bread with Jesus. Talk about a lifetime supply of wine. God was a single parent, too. Me and Her probably have a lot in common. Both of us being single parents and all.

I've come to believe that you've got to have a good philosophy in life. Your own personal mission statement. My philosophy is, the best way in the world to be is not to know nothing, have nothing, wonder about nothing, care about nothing, or expect nothing, because if you don't have nothing and you don't expect nothing, then you've got nothing to disappoint you. And the best place in the world to live is a place where nobody else knows nothing, or has nothing, or got nothing, or wants nothing, or expects nothing, 'cause then you don't even know what you haven't even got, 'cause nobody else haven't even got nothing either. And then you feel good. Really good. You got nothing to lose when you've got nothing.

I developed my philosophy because I was a bit depressed for a long time. I was going to go down to the St. John's harbour front and throw myself over. I got to the wharf and, thank heavens, at the last minute I realized that I couldn't throw myself in and do away with myself because I can't swim. If you can't swim and you throw yourself over the wharf and you drown, it's not really a choice. If you want to drown yourself you have to be able to decide whether to swim or not. And even if you could swim and wanted to throw yourself into the harbour, St. John's is not the place to do it. All of that pollution would give you a really bad infection. Probably kill you.

I went to a psychiatrist. It's frigging excellent. Seeing a psychiatrist is better than being married. He gets paid to sit down and listen to me talk about myself for a whole hour, and he's not allowed to read the paper or watch TV while he's doing it. He's got to look interested whether he really is or not. The worst thing in the world to have is no one to talk to. I've got so many words in my head that my mouth opens up and the words all fall out, like so many Rice Krispies, all over the floor. The psychiatrist tries to talk to me but I won't listen. "I'm OK, you're OK," he says. I say, "I'm dysfunctional, so frig off." He wants me to get in touch with my inner child. I told him I'm from Newfoundland. I was raised on salt beef, salt pork and salt fish. If I've got an inner child he's pickled by now.

So, I'm in my 40s. I hope I make it to 90. If the PMS doesn't kill me. I should not go out in public when I have the PMS. I should lock myself in a box twenty thousand leagues under the sea, which I tried to do. Which is why the cod perished. I know what gives me PMS: how expensive it is to have to go buy all of that feminine protection stuff once a month. Tampons are taxed because the government labels them under cosmetics. Sure. I always powder my nose with a pad. All that money for a box of pads and there ain't no prize in the bottom of the box. CBC should do a documentary on the secret Tampax Tribe of our modern culture. Once a month we go to the store and stand stupefied before the dazzling array of feminine protection we see before us. Slim, extra-slim, regular, super, deodorant, non- deodorant, with applicator, without applicator, plastic applicator, cardboard applicator, panty liners, oval, thong, long, thin, minis, maxis, maxis with wings. Do we wear it or fly it home? Women are reluctant to ask the boyfriend to run to the store for a box of pads. He's liable to come home with Brillo, or SOS. It's so confusing.

I myself don't have a boyfriend. I have trouble hanging on to a man. I don't know why. It's not like I'm looking for much. I just want to get married.

I used to go out a lot. Life was exciting. Once, I remember getting this call, spur of the moment. I was home. It was late. It was 3 o'clock in the morning. I said, "Hello," and in dulcet tones he said, "Hey, baby. I just got back into town. I can't wait to see you. I'm at the Delta, room 306." I got there in no time. What a night we had. Dim lights. Flickering candles. Romantic music. It wasn't until the sun came up that he realized he had dialed the wrong number. Nothing to me. I introduced myself and left.

I used to get my heart broken 10 times a week. I'd meet a really nice guy and he'd always tell me he was going to call me in the morning. But he never did. They never do. Guys always say they'll call you in the morning but they don't really mean it. It's just something they say so you'll let go of their legs.

They've got condoms everywhere these days, even in the women's bathroom. They come in all kinds of colours. Pink passion. Neon green. That's nice to see coming at you from out of the dark. A green pickle that glows. Now they come in new extra-large sizes. All the guys buy them. Never mind that when they get them home and put them on they've got to tie a knot on top.

Welfare Goddess

Far be it me to judge about who I see sneaking in her back door in the middle of the night. If the welfare finds out she'll be in for it. That feller next door, he's another hard case. He's been off with a bad back for the past six months. He's walking pretty straight there now, though, by the looks of him. I wouldn't say nothing to nobody about it. I'm only your friendly neighbourhood Welfare Goddess. I sees everything. I knows nothing.

Just because I'm on the welfare doesn't mean I got to go around dressed like a streel. I take a lot of pride in my appearance. All of my clothing is purchased, one hundred percent polyester, at WalMart and then I has it tailor-made for me over at the M & B auto parts and crafts store. I has my alterations done on one side of the store, and has a lube job while I'm waiting.

I only popped out from under the table to have a smoke. Only I forgot, I'm after quitting. Now what did I go and do a thing like that for? Now I'm only gonna live longer.

If it wasn't for the Valium, my dear, I'd be on the drugs. Why shouldn't I be on the drugs? Everyone else I knows is on the drugs. I got a sister is on the Prozac, my Aunt is on the Zoloft, the kids is on the Ritalin, my cousin is on the Ativan, Father's on the EI, and Mudder's on the back porch cause that's where she smokes at.

What's that, Dolly, my honey? No, my honey, you can't come out. No, my baby. Get back in under the table. Stay in! Stay in! Stay in!

So, how are you? Fine, I hope. I'm fine too. I don't really care how you are, to tell you the truth. It's just something I says so I can talk about myself. I'm good though. I'm good. I'm good. I'm good. I'm really frigging good. Up three times a night with the triplets, I'm good and tired. I got a hole in the roof, leaking to bejesus; I'm good and wet. The welfare cheque is late again; I'm good and upsot. And, I'm right in the middle of me cycle; I'm good and depressed. If I gets any gooder, I'm going down and jumping off the good goddamn wharf.

What my honey? No, ye youngsters can't come out. No, my baby. Ye can't come out to play. Ye got to stay under there because if the welfare finds out I'm babysitting under the table they'll cut me off for sure.

No, I'm good for someone having a nervous breakdown. I just likes to sit home and count the cracks in the stucco: 247. Reminds me of my wedding night. Poor old Harold. Things are just not the same since he fell off the scaffold and broke his back and died. He was never the same after that. But still, death is a never-ending virtue, but only if you're dead, cause look at me, I'm alive, but I'd be better off dead, but I'm good though!

Dolly, sweetheart, pass mommy out her pills, will you? No, not them ones, honey. That's for my bad head. No, not them ones either. That's for my ulcer. No, not them ones either. Those are for when I turns into a nutbar, and starts to run around up and down the street, ripping off me clothes till I'm stark naked, and screeching like a banshee. No, I need my pink pills for when I feel too happy. The psychiatrist told me that the worst thing in the world for someone in my situation is to feel too happy. It just means you're in for a bigger letdown later on when life starts crashing in on you like a ton of bricks. No, the best way to feel good is to be in a constant state of chronic depression.

I should never have gotten married the second time around in the first place. Then I would not have ended up on the welfare. Always a bride, never a bridesmaid, that's me. But now, here I am, I get my child support payments from my second husband twice removed from society, cause not only are we divorced but he's in jail. But the child support payments get deducted off my welfare cheque, because they calls that income, and then we can't eat because we got no money. We sits around the supper table all day long looking at pictures of macaroni and cheese.

I didn't start out in life planning to be on the welfare, you know. When I was in Grade 3 and Miss asked us, what did we want to be when we grew up? I never put up my hand and said, Miss! Miss! I wants to be on the welfare, Miss! I coulda been somebody you know. I coulda been a contender. I used to be in show business. I was a Pronouncer. You know the announcements you hear over the intercom at WalMart? Attention, WalMart shoppers? That was me.

But now I'm on the welfare. Every time I get something, I got to lose something. That's the law of life when you're on the welfare. Get something, lose something. The other day I was walking down the street, and I saw a nickel on the sidewalk. And I couldn't help myself. I leaned over and picked it up and put it in my pocket. And, sure enough! The next month they had a whole extra nickel took off me cheque. Your life is not your own when you're on the welfare cause they watches you. They spies on you. I know they got me bugged. I won't even sit down on the toilet because I don't know what's looking back up at me.

That's the way of the world. Get something. Lose something. Get something. Lose something. Look at me. I'm the perfect living example. Got married. Lost me virginity. Got the youngsters. Lost me figure. Got the welfare. Lost me mind.

Sometimes I think there's something wrong with me because I hates me youngsters. My oldest just moved back in with me, her and her new husband, and her new baby. And her new husband is newer than her new baby. I can't hold my head up down to the bingo at all. And that's not the worst of it. She's only going around breastfeeding. Letting it all hang out everywhere she goes with a youngster latched on to the front of her. He must be gonna be a deep-sea diver when he grows up, he don't come up for air. Who would want to breastfeed a youngster as long as there's a perfectly good can of Carnation milk up into the cupboard?

Don't be talking about my youngsters. Sharon and Nick are always fighting over something, and it's terrible what happened to Cassie. And Victor and Nikki is after been married five or six times and that's just the times they were married to each other. Brittany is singing in a strip club … oh, wait a minute … that's not my youngsters…that's *The Young and the Restless*.

My mind is falling out. Last week I took the twins to the wrong school by mistake and they spent all day down there talking French with the Catholics and I had to have them exorcised.

And I'm not well, you know. Now you knows I never goes to the doctor unless I'm dying on my feet. And I am not one to talk about my problems to other people. No, my dear. I never opens my mouth about my problems. I wouldn't open my mouth to complain. Don't be talking, that's my motto. Everything that comes out of me is true; it's not just an insinuisation. I am not one to confabucate or talk loose. My business is my business as far as I'm circumcised. Even when my poor old husband, Harold, God rest his soul, when he went through that bout of impudence. Oh my, he was right impudent, and he had to have his prostitute gland taken out. I never opened my mouth about it. Even when my vericloset veins got all puffed out and burst open, it was nothing to me. I hates the doctors. Who wants them coming at you, wanting to test your reflections with a hammer and putting a thermostat in your mouth and palpitrating your bosoms? I told that doctor, I said, I already had my tonsillectomies out, thank you very much. Now take that barometer off my arm before I flattens you. Oh, yes, I told him and I was very pacific about it too. I pacifically told him, if you tries to get me up on that table, my son, putting my feet up in them stirrups so you can go speculating, I'll give you such a kick in the privates, my son, you'll be singing alcopoco for a year.

The worst thing is trying to make ends meet. My God, the price of gas is gone some high, isn't it? Next thing you know there won't be no one able to afford to drive a car anymore, or have a snowmobile or an ATV. We'll have to go back to the old days, back to horse-and-buggy days. And so we should, too, go back to the old days when everyone had a horse and there was no need of any welfare cause if you were starving to death you ate the horse. There was no need for welfare because everyone was poor back then. That was the way of the world. You were poor. Unless you were rich. But if you weren't rich, you were poor, and you made no odds about it. There was no Valium back then. If you were poor you had no time to be depressed because you had to work all the time. That's all poor people did back then. Work. And the more they worked, the more poor off they were. That's a queer thing. Back then the poor people had to go around working all the time, and nowadays the poor people got no work to work at.

There was no such thing as government back then, and if there was, you didn't know who they were or have nothing to do with them. You got what you got, and you had what you had, and if anyone came along and tried to govern you, you let the geese out to peck him to death. Nowadays it's all government and all the government is, is cuts. Cuts, cuts, cuts. they comes along and cuts anything they likes. It's all cut this and cut that, cut, cut, cut. Well, they won't get to cut nothing else off me cause I'll cut off both my arms and then I'll cut off both my legs and then I'll cut the eyes out of my head and then I'll chop off my own head and sit on it, and then I'll light up a smoke and burn the lips right off myself. Then they won't cut anything else off me.

We're too political these days. Going on and on about how we gave the world John Crosbie and we gave the world Clyde Wells and we gave the world Brian Peckford and Brian Tobin. We gave them to the world because we didn't want them no more.

The taxes got us kilt. They thinks they got us tricked, with the harmonized sales tax. I don't feel very harmonious. I feels like smacking someone in the mouth. Got the GST and the HST. All it is, is a tax rolled onto the tax, a tax

tax onto the tax. I went into the store the other day to buy a box of tacks. So I had one box of tacks at $1 plus the real tax, plus the hidden tax, plus the other hidden tax tacked on to the tax, next thing you knows, a box of tacks is $143.

And I hates that frigging dibit card thingy they got out now. Hates it. You knows, that dibit card thingy. Goes in and pays with a dibit card. No one takes a cheque anymore. The worst thing about the dibit cards is, they don't work unless you got money in the bank. Who the frig got money in the bank? Back in the old days you could write a cheque even if you didn't have money in the bank, cause you knew by the time the cheque cleared you *would* have money in the bank, and then you could write another cheque on the money that was *going* to be in the bank, so you were always a step ahead of yourself. You could write a cheque for the groceries on Wednesday, get paid Thursday, put the money in the bank on Friday, that went through on Monday, so you could write another cheque on Tuesday, and have the money for the groceries on Wednesday! You can't go in to a store with a dibit card and tell them, that's all right, my love. The money will be in the bank at the end of the week. No, my dear. Who the frig can afford to buy anything if you got to have money in the bank!

But I totally and pacifically agrees with all this Sunday shopping rigamarole. They got the liquor stores open on Sundays now, and it's the right proper thing, too. Where in heaven's name do you think the church buys all the liquor from? No, not from heaven. From the liquor store. The blood of Christ comes out of a bottle and that bottle comes out of a liquor store. That same liquor store which is now open on Sundays, doing the work of the Lord, selling the

Lord's blood. That store is God's liquor store, and God wants me to get a bottle of wine there every day of the week and twice on Sundays. Just like confession.

But, I rues the day, yes, my dear, rues the day I had electricity put in the house. I don't care what they says about Lower Churchill Falls going to save the day. I'm tortured with the light bills. Look at the light bill I got this month. On the one side they're telling me I owes them up in the quadruple digits, and on the other side they're asking me if I wants to make them a donation. So the poor people can pay their light bills. Me! Make them a donation. I don't have a cent. I've done everything I know how to cut back. I don't even have a light bulb in the fridge anymore. I can't see what I'm eating half the time. I could die with the food poisoning any minute. And the power company is raking in the billions and billions. I sent them a Hallmark card of congratulations. It says, Dear Light and Power. Congratulations on all your profits. And, I'm not paying my light bill, so frig off. Don't talk to me about Lower Churchill Falls. Why do they want to Lower Churchill Falls? Leave it where it's at. Next thing they'll want to move the Upper Gullies to Middle Cove. I don't know what hydro has to do with my electricity anyway. Hydro is water, and water is water, and electricity is electricity, and if the government wants to mix water with electricity, they're going to get some jeezly shock. I thinks they're going to have another think coming when they're fried.

That's another thing I misses about the old days. When you could have a drink of water without going to the store to buy it in the bottle. Shocking thing, buying water. Ordinary water is no good anymore. It got to come in a bottle with a label on it. I suppose we got no choice, with all the things in the water these days. The parameciums and the parasites and the bacteria and the tcm's and the tch's and the mcp's. What don't kill you makes you stronger. Or leaves you half dead. Everyone should dig a well and go back to the days when the only thing you bottled was the moonshine. No, my dear, you can't even make your own moonshine no more, they'll haul you off for that. Can't even get drunk anymore without someone else wanting to stick their nose in it. Back in the old days it was no odds if you got drunk. If you got drunk you fell down and slept it off where you lay and then you got up and went home and kicked the horse.

Oh well. I suppose we'll do all right under Danny Williams. The new messiah. We got to find out when his birthday is, so we'll know when to celebrate Christmas. He got the Umbilical Accord for us, anyway. He plays a good game of Bingo. He won the jackpot and he wasn't too shy to sing out about it. I only hope we gets our cheque soon. I suppose they're still dividing it up. I hope they mails it out cause I got a letter from the finance company saying they're coming to take the stove away. They can go ahead and take it for all I'm circumcised, nothing to me. I'm moving to a gravel pit with the Coleman stove and a can of beans.

I do the best I can. I babysits under the table. And why the frig not? That's what all the politicians do; deals under the table. Last election they knocked the legs clear off the frigging table. Thank God I'm lucky enough to even have a table over my head. We can't blame the government for wanting to come and take everything. That's the way of the world. Get something. Lose something. Get something. Lose something. We're the ones voted them in. Well, no. Not me. I wouldn't give anyone my vote, cause God only knows what they'd want to come and take away then!

Poor old Harold. If he was still alive, I'd kill him.

I am a Newfoundlander

Hello. My name is Berni and I am a Newfoundlander, except, I'm sorry, I forgot. We've had an official name change and we have to use the full name now. So, anyway, my name is Bernardine Anne Teraz Stapleton and I am from Newfoundland and Labrador. I was born in Labrador and I grew up in Newfoundland, on the Burin Peninsula, which gives me dual citizenship status. My heart is pure Labradorite and the blood red ochre flows through my veins.

According to Stats Canada it is a little-known, well-known fact that we watch more TV, laugh more, smoke more, drink more, give more to charity more, have way more sex more, eat the worst kind of food more, work longer weeks for less pay more, and club way more seals more, than anyone else in all the rest of Canada.

Don't ask me to talk funny, or say, "The toid is high," and don't tell me that all us little Newfoundlanders are so quaint and cute and frigging funny because some of us are crooked and cranky and contrary and really freaking hard to look at, if you ask me. Take a look around. And, don't ask me if I know your third cousin twice removed whose last name you can't recall, but who came to Noo-fund-lund once for a holiday three years ago. Or maybe it was Cape Breton. Because some people can't tell the difference.

If people want to come to Newfoundland and kiss a codfish, then that's their own fault. Wanting to be Screeched in and kiss a codfish. Oh no, we're not allowed to fish the cod, but it's OK to neck with it.

Unapologetic, I refuse to wipe my lips on the coattails of the *Globe and Mail* and say, "I'm sorry," yet again for all the things that Canada had to do for us. We did more for Canada than Canada ever did for us. We gave Canada the fish, the Churchill Falls, the best of our resources and human talent. If they ask for anything else, I'll give them the finger.

And no matter what they say, it's not that there is no work in Newfoundland and Labrador. It's just that we're all so busy going around laughing from being the happy frigging province, going around laughing more, smoking more, drinking more, having all that sex more, watching TV more, eating the worst kind of food more, working longer weeks for less pay more, and clubbing way more seals more, frankly, my dear, we're all beat to a snot.

Maclean's magazine had a big survey which went right across the country, and they found out that in Newfoundland we watch more TV and have way more sex than anyone else in all the rest of Canada. There's no mystery to it. We have more sex than anyone else in all the rest of Canada because everything in Newfoundland happens half an hour later. So, we have an extra 30 minutes more than anyone else in which to have sex. And, after you're done having sex you've got to find something to do for the other 27 minutes, so you turn on the TV. Many a wife goes into the bedroom and says to her husband, "Is that the clicker up in underneath the covers, or are you happy to see me?" It's usually the clicker.

Newfoundland is the promised land. It was on the news the other day that they found another boatload of those poor refugees out off the coast, hanging off the side of an iceberg, half-frozen, half-drowned to death, trying to escape their life of desperation and poverty. They came over on a boat from Cape Breton.

It's a little-known, well-known fact that Newfoundland is the centre of the universe. It is the centre of the universe, because when you live in Newfoundland you are always exactly halfway from everywhere else in the world. So, no matter where in the world that you want to go, you're already halfway there. Which means, you don't have to bother going anywhere cause you're already halfway there. You're only going to get halfway there and you've got to turn around and come halfway back again. Stay home out of it. You're better off.

Touring Newfoundland is an eye-opening experience. You could end up going anywhere. You could end up doing anything. You could go to Port de Grave and dig your own. You can go to Isle aux Morts. That's where you go if you'd rather be dead. In Croque they're all born dead. In Conche they're all brain dead. In Keel's Cove they're keeled over. In Burnt Harbour they're fried. In Baie d'Espoir they're desperate. In Dildo - well, they're really frigging happy in Dildo. And I'm not even going to get into the fact that Joe Batt's Arm is halfway up Hibb's Hole.

It's no good to move away, to move out to Alberta somewhere. You will only whine and complain and pine away for the rest of your days until you can get back home again. You can't ever really leave Newfoundland because you are born with an invisible umbilical cord that can never be cut. The apron string that will never let go. I know Newfoundlanders who've been living on the mainland for 50 years and they still think it's only temporary. Even the dead won't leave Newfoundland. They die. They see the white light. They say, "What! Go to heaven? When I can stay in Newfoundland and camp in a gravel pit!" That's why Newfoundland is maggoty with ghosts and haunts. They won't frigging move on! Newfoundlanders are just like caplin. The caplin is the only fish that won't swim the other way when it sees a net. It cheerfully rolls up on shore, hops into your waiting bucket and then happily jumps out into the frying pan, thinking it's having a wonderful adventure. Just like a Newfoundlander. Doesn't know he's sitting on the stove till his arse is on fire. We are like the noble salmon, the only fish that could be swimming around, happy and free, frolicking in the Atlantic. But it insists on being miserable, trying to swim upstream, against the current, toward the nets and the fishermen and the poachers so it can lay an egg by a rock and get eaten by a bear. It's in the bear's gullet, on its way to being bear poo, and all it can think is, "My God, it's some good to be home." It is genetically programmed into us that we have to roll ashore and beach once more before we die. Because we are the real old NewfoundLabradorites.

Motherhood

I have a broken heart. The man in my life just left me. He packed his bags … well, no. Actually, I packed his bags for him. Me and my Mom and Dad packed his bags for him, did his laundry, ironing, mending, shopping, folding, sorting and packing, because he can't manage to find his own underwear to save his life, not even when they're lying on the bedroom floor looking at him.

But I digress. The man in my life sat me down recently and told me that we had grown apart. He said his life was taking a different path than mine and that it was time to let him go. Then he asked me for 20 bucks so he could go to the movies with his friends. Off he went, out the door, without a backward glance toward where I lay on the living floor, crying and smoking and clutching the clicker so I could watch *Coronation Street* through my copious tears.

I thought of the old expression, if you love something, set it free. If it comes back, it's yours. If it doesn't, hunt it down and make it feel guilty.

So, he's gone. Twenty-one years we've been together. I've loved him, supported him, cleaned up his mess and changed his diapers. Yes, I gave birth to him. He's my son and he just moved to Calgary, where he will live and whine and moan and pine out the rest of his days until he can beach once more upon the noble shores of Newfoundland, along with the rest of the caplin and salmon and fools of the sea.

He's gone. The only thing I can wonder is, how soon can I decently change all the locks and turn his bedroom into a home office?

He was born, kicking and screaming, already wearing a pair of skates with a pack of smokes tucked into his diaper, and a hockey stick clutched in one chubby fist. When he left home he was wearing much the same thing.

I miss the days of forking over 20 bucks every time I turned around. Twenty bucks for a movie. Twenty bucks for girls. Twenty bucks for beer. Twenty bucks for girls. I knew I should have had a girl. I could have used the extra income.

I think back on the best time I ever had in my life, when I was pregnant. You get so much attention. You're blissfully happy because you're blissfully ignorant about what lies ahead. You can't waddle down the street without someone coming up to you and poking you in the stomach like they're kneading dough. Little old ladies stand around and talk about you like you're not even there.

"Oh, she's carrying high. It's going to be a boy." "No, she's carrying low, it's going to be a girl." "My dear, I had 21, didn't even know I was having them."

I knew I was having mine. I didn't know any better. I took Lamaze classes. Amazing Lamaze. They teach you how to have a natural painless childbirth. Hello, natural painless childbirth. Halfway through my delivery I tried to kill my husband. I said to him, I said, you tell me what is natural about lying up here on a cold, hard table with my legs spread out in a pair of stirrups. My body is racked with pain as the contractions rip me from stem to stern, and bunch of strangers stand around and stare at my privates. And my husband sits and holds my hand and says, "There, now. That's not so bad, is it?" I said, "You! You and your 'let's make whoopee.' You did this to me. Well, you get up here and shit out a basketball because I'm not doing it anymore." I think that while the wife is having the baby, the husband should have a root canal with no anesthetic. So he can better share in the beautiful miracle of childbirth.

Everyone lies to you when you're pregnant. It's a complete boldfaced false advertising conspiracy. Nobody tells you the truth. They don't tell you that after you have your new baby, you've got to take it home with you. Nobody tells you you'll be so tired you'll throw yourself in front of a moving truck just so you can lie down for five minutes. That's just one of the joys of having your new baby home with you. Here's another joy: your very first stretch marks. The front of your stomach looks like a cheese grater. Why doesn't anyone tell you that stretch marks don't ever go away? They'll be a kind of a purple-bluey colour for a while, and then they'll settle into a doughy pasty texture, but they won't ever go away. After a while you'll forget they're there. Kind of like the way you can forget your husband is there while you're having sex and making out the grocery list in your head. (It was a very short list in my case).

My friend Gloria Swelchburg had rose vines tattooed all over her stretch marks to try to hide them, but I wouldn't recommend it. It looks like she sat on a hedge. Her husband won't go near her unless he's got the clippers.

One time I put the baby down somewhere and forgot where he was. I got up for the four and the five and the six o'clock feedings, and then I fell asleep standing up by the stove. I couldn't sit down, my episiotomy was too tight. They had me stitched up so tight I peed sideways for a year. Anyway, I found the baby when I did a load of laundry. He was in the laundry basket. Thank God new babies are tougher than they look.

All anyone has to do to stop teenage pregnancy is to show them a picture of my naked boy. My youthful figure is gone for good. You should see my boobs. I don't even have to get out of bed to breastfeed anymore. I can sling a tit over the side of the crib and reel it back in when I'm done. Convenient, though.

Then I had the baby blues. Postpartum depression. It's like PMS, but nuclear PMS. Go beat something up. You'll feel a lot better.

I had a total nervous breakdown. One night I looked at myself in the bathroom mirror. I had a shitty diaper over one shoulder, baby vomit all over the other shoulder. I hadn't washed my hair in three days and there was gum in it. I was so tired I was asleep with my eyes open, and the bags under my eyes were hanging down to my chin. And I thought, you know, I'm never going to drive through Paris in a sports car with the warm wind in my hair.

Just hope you don't get the hemorrhoids like I did. They were the size of basketballs. I was three feet taller sitting down than when I was standing up.

No, no one tells you that after all of your suffering and sacrifice, the little infant grows up to break your heart. He throws you over for some 18-year-old tart with her belly button pierced.

I miss the child he was. I wonder about the man he will become. He told me he was going to take care of me in my old age. He told me he'll put an apartment over his garage just for me. I suppose by then I will be the one looking for 20 bucks every other day. Twenty bucks for cat food, for

Depends, for Polident and beer. Well, he's a hockey player, so by then both of us will have dentures, so we can share the Polident and beer.

The One Thing

Jimmy McShaney says that at midnight on Christmas Eve all the animals in the barn will fall to their knees in honour of the birth of sweet baby Jesus. My best friend Cindy says I should be careful about going into the barn alone with Jimmy McShaney, or with any boy for that matter, because boys are only after one thing. I don't know what that one thing could be, but the thought of it gives me a queer sweet feeling in the pit of my stomach. Cindy knows all about the one thing because even though we are only in Grade 6 she has a different boyfriend every other month, and takes them under the overpass to do mysterious things with them. She is a woman of the world because she was the first girl in our class to smoke, to get her period, and to wear a training bra. My own breasts are not yet in training, as far as I know a period is a punctuation mark, and I have had zero boyfriends. Cindy tolerates me because I cadge cigarette butts from out of my father's ashtray and always let her have the last draw. I am dying to know all about the one thing but I will not give Cindy the satisfaction of asking. Jimmy McShaney is a year behind me in school, only in Grade 5, so maybe he's the one who should be nervous about the one thing instead of me. We've known each other ever since I can remember. He always smells of hay and cows and hand-scrubbed clothing, a combination of odours that also gives me the queer sweet sensation in my tummy. It is the McShaney's barn that holds the great allure of the animals kneeling at midnight and the possibility of the one thing.

Getting to the barn for the midnight miracle will take some considerable deceit, dishonesty and duplicity on my part. It's no odds at all to Jimmy McShaney whether he goes to the barn at midnight or mid-morning. It's all the same to him. He comes from a very odd family. They seem to like each other. They all come and go as they please, he and his brother and his two sisters, turning up at their home at the same time for chores and meals and bedtimes, laughing and chatting and talking to each other as polite as strangers at a church social. I long for a life such as that. It isn't Jimmy McShaney's father who will be loaded by 10 o'clock on Christmas Eve night, insisting that the rest of us truck off to the deadly boring Midnight Mass so he can stay home to drink and to inadvertently mangle this year's race car set while setting it up. He'll be wearing the Christmas tree by the time we get home. The house will be filled with cigarette smoke, the smuggled Christmas rum will be open on the kitchen table, the turkey will be stuffed and ready to go in the oven, and the living room will be maggoty with noisy drunken neighbours who won't lurch home until three or four in the morning, the very same neighbours that he hates and passionately maligns the rest of the year.

How to get out of the deadly Midnight Mass. Surely witnessing a genuine Christmas Eve miracle will be a much more enlightening and spiritual experience than surviving the half-hour homily by Father Penney. Father Penney is our parish priest and he will not allow any happy hymns, much less anything like a Folk Mass, which we hear is all the rage in St. John's, with priests and nuns frolicking at the altar with guitars and blessing real live animals. Sweet Baby Jesus was born in a barn, so it seems to make more sense to celebrate his birthday there rather than in the over-crowded overheated pews of the church. There is no adult in my world who would find this acceptable. Not counting my mother, who is very lovely and kind, but who carries as much authority in our home as me. None.

There is the option of faking the flu and climbing out the bathroom window, but that runs the risk of being checked on, and worse, not being allowed to go on the Christmas Day visiting jaunt to see relatives and friends, and to gorge on cherry cakes, nips of sherry and more importantly, to collect more presents. There is the option of sneaking out of the church during the deadly Midnight Mass and returning in time for communion, but the distance between the church and the McShaney's barn is greater than three miles. In any case, my absence would be noted, if not by my mother then by one of my two fickle younger brothers. There is also the risk of Sister putting me in the choir to fill out the front row because I am the right height, although I am not allowed to sing, only to move my lips.

It is hopeless. I am hopeless.

Relief comes in the form of Jimmy McShaney's mother, who telephones my house to ask if she should pack the kids a lunch to take on their little midnight miracle adventure. Thank the good Lord it is my mother who answers the phone. She tells me she will drop me off at the McShaney's barn before the deadly Midnight Mass and pick me up on the return trip. She threatens the two fickle brothers with the image of the annual race car set, mangled or not, resting on the floor beneath the tree of an underprivileged family (of which we know many). If either of the two fickle brothers gets spitey and tattles anyway, she will say I went to the deadly Midnight Mass with one of the McShaney girls so I could help take up the collection.

The night sky is black with startling stars aglimmer in the frigid cold. The air inside the barn is merely freezing with steamy spouts rising from the cows. Jimmy McShaney and I soon warm up as we nestle in the hay among the confused sheep, goats, barn cats and the dog with one ear. We warm up in the stink of all that animal poop, but we don't care. Neither one of us has a watch so we have no way of knowing when midnight comes or goes. We eat the exquisite ham and cheese sandwiches made just for this occasion with all store-bought stuff and smothered in mayonnaise. We eat and then watch our breath hang in the air, talking of everything and nothing in the manner of polite strangers chatting at a church social.

And then the one thing happens. Jimmy McShaney's mittened hand reaches for my gloved fingers. We hold bulky hands and pretend we are Mary and Joseph. The heifer due to be slaughtered in the new year kneels at our feet and we pretend it is Sweet Baby Jesus. I am young but wise enough to know that I have never been so happy in my entire life, and that I will never know such a moment again.

Laugh, I Thought I'd Die

Bernadette

The time is always coming for something. Be quiet or you'll wake the dead, is what they told us when we were youngsters. But you are supposed to wake the dead. Wake: the watch over the body of a dead person through the night, before the burial. Friends come to see you. "Oh, she looks wonderful." "Oh, she looks better now than she ever did." A real professional does your makeup for you. Everyone comes to say goodbye. They have drinks, and say the Rosary, and have more drinks. They tell nice stories about you, even if they have to make them up.

Wake: to become active after being dormant. Well. I was always a morning person. I loved to take on the day. "I'll be dead long enough," was my motto.

Wake: to stir up. Wake! The track left by a boat passing through the water. The area behind any moving thing. All the flotsam and jetsam you leave trailing behind you.

I remember some of it. Some flotsams. Some jetsams.

In the beginning, there was me. Bernadette. I am named after St. Bernadette of Lourdes. That's how I met the Pope. It was a miracle because I'm from Lourdes too. Lourdes in Newfoundland. A second Bernadette from a second Lourdes. Make no wonder the Pope took time out from his big worldwide PR tour to come and meet me.

I know everything about St. Bernadette the original, the one from France. She was really sweet and shy and cute and starved for attention. One day while she was out for a walk, who should appear in front of her but the Holy Virgin Mary Mother of God. Only Bernadette could see the Virgin.

No one else could, not even if they squinted. The Holy Virgin Mary Mother of God told Bernadette all kinds of fabulous secrets and showed her where to dig up a holy spring. Bernadette lived out the rest of her life being extremely popular and very well known and a very successful saint. So you can see why the Pope would be anxious to meet me. I was Bernadette. I lived in Lourdes. I wasn't yet officially a saint but I worked very hard all the time to be as saintly as possible. Although, sorrowfully, many times my actions were misunderstood. This is not an uncommon frustration for budding saints. I did not try to drown my brother when he was three. Granny did not have to smack me in the head as often as she did. But it is not uncommon for a saint to be smacked in the head. My Lourdes was only a small fishing village hanging off the side of a cliff. I tried many times to dig up a holy spring, but there was just no digging through solid rock. Granny did not have to rant about what I did to her potato garden. I couldn't find a holy spring, and I never once saw the Holy Virgin Mary Mother of God, not even when I squinted. But I knew that as soon as the Pope laid eyes on me, he would immediately see that inside of me there beat the heart of a real true saint.

He came in a helicopter, descending from on high, sliding down a silver rope ladder, wearing shiny robes that sparkled in the sun, and blue suede shoes. He saw me at once. He said, "Well, looky here. I just clapped my eyes on a real true saint. Little lady, you have got to come to Rome and live in the Vatican with me. You've got to be where people can love you. People here can't possibly appreciate a real true saint like you. You have suffered enough. I can tell by looking at you. You have got to come with me and live in a state of Graceland."

He made Granny say a million Hail Marys. He was in such a good mood, he cancelled Purgatory, and he cancelled Limbo too. Null and void. All the little dead babies, null and void. He sold Granny his autograph.

Saints do have to suffer for a while, of course. They have to be tortured, mutilated, sometimes boiled in oil, or burned. But God fixes it so they don't feel too much pain. And there is no such thing as an ugly saint. Every saint ever seen in the movies is famous and gorgeous.

Granny never felt anything in a regular way. She only ever had royal headaches, or a royally good day. She often had a royal pain right where her left breast used to be. Which meant, a pain in her heart. When they cut her breast off, her heart was too close to the surface, and more easily hurt. I didn't care about her old breasts. I didn't want any breasts. Saints don't have breasts. Saints don't need breasts. The Pope told me so. He said, " You're better off if you don't have any. Mark my words! Remember St. Agatha? Lovely girl. Came from a good Sicilian family. What a little sweetheart. Happy as a lark. But she was being courted by a lecherous judge who wanted to have his wicked way with her. Nudge-nudge wink-wink. When she refused him he chopped off her breasts. The moral of the story is, it's best not to have any breasts at all in the first place."

Granny called her breasts "tits." The Pope did not come all the way from Rome to hear her say "tit" but she didn't care.

The Pope issued a new Papal Bull. He declared the year of the Great Indulgence. Easy peasy. You do a good deed.

Or, you give something up. You quit smoking. Or you suffer in silence about something without whining. You offer each little sacrifice up to God, and for each one you are granted an Indulgence. You save up your Indulgences just like you save up Aeroplan Points on Air Canada, and before you know it you've got a free ticket for the trip to heaven.

Granny always said she indulged me too much. But she was sure jealous when the Pope gave me a special teacup. His visage on a cup, handmade by blind nuns in Vatican City, blessed by a crippled Cardinal and sanctified by His Grace himself. The Pope in a cup.

When they were wheeling me into the operating room, it struck me. I would finally achieve my dream of sainthood. The pain would elevate me to a greater spiritual level. The scars would distinguish me as a martyr. I begged them to let me stay awake, to have it done without any anesthetic. I wanted to suffer as much as possible, to offer it up. For every sacrifice I offered up, the Pope would issue a special Breast Indulgence to women everywhere, absolving the breasts of all sin, purifying the cells, reducing breast time spent in Purgatory. My daughter would be safe because I gave up my breast to save hers. And George wouldn't mind having to put up with me. Everyone would say, " Oh but he could never leave her. She's such a saint."

It might be nice to have a heart that pops out of place when it's convenient. When feelings grow too strong. When you want to show someone that you love them, you can let them hold your heart. In all the pictures you see of her, the Holy Virgin Mary's heart is always floating around outside of her body. Proof of all the love she feels.

Flotsams and jetsams. The first time George and I did it after my surgery, I was in the bathroom getting undressed, putting on my nightgown in the dark, fumbling in the shadows, hiding. And then the door swung open behind me and there's George. I've got my drawers half off and my big old flannel nightie up over my head. And he just came right on in, so quiet and shy. And then, him and me, we looked at it, where it used to be, at what was left, the flatness of me. And then we, you know. And it was like the first time ever. And the whole time I was thinking about how much I love his socks. How much I love to wash his socks. His socks are washed, dried, ironed, sorted, rolled, and tucked away, lined up according to colour and texture. I was thinking how happy I was to know I would always be around to do that for him.

I've never seen the Virgin Mary Mother of God. Not even once. Not even when I squinted very hard. And at the end it burned. It burned like Joan of Arc. My heart was strong, and so firmly in its proper place. But a strong heart is no good when everything else is failing. I look back and see my wake behind me but I don't remember everything. Not all of it. I remember the Pope. He didn't come to see me, of course. He came to bless the fleet. I remember that part. The sun beating down on Lourdes while His Grace blessed the little fleet, the boats sailing in, their wakes trailing behind them. And I was holding Granny's hand, a little girl, with my breasts and all my brief life still before me.

Granny

Some said I looked better than I did in real life. They had me done up like a tart. I wanted to smack someone.

I wish they had cut the other one off while they were at it. Nothing but a nuisance. After I had the kids my tits were all used up anyway. Not a gig left in them. I told that doctor when he had me on the operating table, lop the other one off too. Two, two, two tits for the price of one. But would he listen to me? What do they know? Nothing. That's what they know. Told me the lump was nothing to worry about. That's what killed Bernadette's mother. Should have had her tits lopped off right from the start and she'd be alive today.

Never wash your hair when you're on your period. It'll bring on the flu. Never wash your hair and go outside. It'll bring on the pneumonia. Never sit on cold concrete. It'll bring on disease of the kidneys. Don't take too many hot baths. The hot water stirs up the cancer cells. One hot bath a week is plenty. And even then, one tubful is good enough for four or five people. Trim your hair on the full moon. It'll grow faster. Don't ever shave your legs or you'll end up as hairy as a monkey. There is nothing in life that a good hot bread poultice can't cure. And if your frigging doctor won't listen to you, chop your own frigging tit off and shove it down his throat. I'm spinning in my grave.

I was a young cutie-pie myself. Not too hard on the eyes at all. Six youngsters changed all that. I no sooner weaned one off the tit then there was another one ready to latch on. Nowadays it's all hoity toity, everyone's into how the mother's own milk is so healthy. They turn up their nose at you if you don't go all natural. Everyone goes around with a youngster latched on to the front of them, letting it all hang out everywhere they goes. Back in my day it was only poor people who did that. Rich people had cans of Carnation milk to feed the youngsters with. Nice feeling, though, a youngster latched onto you. All soft and tingly. Nice big rush when your milk let go.

What did I ever know about checking your tits and Pap smears and mammograms and the like? The only grams I ever knew about were telegrams. I think they dreams up half of those tests cause they don't know what else to be doing with you. I had all my babies at home with the midwife. The first time I ever went to the hospital was to have my gallbladder out. And even then, even now, my motto is that there's nothing that a good cup of tea can't fix. A good cup of tea, a hot bread poultice, and a good night's sleep. If that can't fix it, then nothing can, and there's no point whinging about it.

Tits. Titties. Tough titty said the kitty, made the milk taste shitty. Bite my titty. Bosoms. Bazoombas. Honkers, hooters, hootchies. Knockers. Jugs. Udders. Melons. Puppies. Over your shoulder boulder holders.

Back in my day there was no such thing as spirituality. That's a new thing that came out around the time tossed salads came out. In my day you went to church and you got down on your knees and you thanked God and all creation for what little you had.

And when I was pregnant on my youngsters I went to church and I got down on my knees and I prayed to God and all creation. Please God, don't let it be a girl. Let me have boys. Please God, let me have boys. Don't let me have no girls to pass this poison on to.

My tits were brave little tits. I couldn't have asked for a finer pair of tits. They were tits among tits. I've got some mighty fine memories of the old gals. And, I'd just like to say, they are fondly remembered.

I always had long hair. I loved my hair, all braided up and wrapped around my head like I was a little Dutch girl. I missed it after it all fell out. I molted like a hen. Not that I let anyone know it. I wore scarves. I wouldn't let anyone see my naked head. I wouldn't let my daughters see me without my bandanna. Then one day I got caught in the rain, and didn't I get soaking wet. So I trots on home and into the kitchen, hauling the wet scarf from off my head, thinking there's no one around. And lo and behold, unbeknownst to me my daughters are sitting in the kitchen having a cup of tea. Cause there's nothing like a good cup of tea. I looked at them. They looked at me. I wanted to croak right where I stood. All of them looking at me and me as bald as a baby. Bald as an old bald eagle. Then my oldest jumped up and grabbed hold of me and says, "Mom, I never knew how beautiful you are. I couldn't see your face for all the hair." Next thing I know they're jumping up and down and screaming because I'm so frigging gorgeous without all my hair. Laugh, I thought I'd die. I told them not to be so stunned. But I got a bit vain after that. I started sneaking on a dab of rouge and putting on perfume when no one was looking. Now that was living it up. Still. They didn't have to make me look like a tart when I was in the coffin.

Diana

She died of a broken heart. Literally. The force of the collision was so great that it ripped her heart out of place. It was irreparably broken. Her last meal was simple and elegant. A small feast of scrambled eggs and a glass of red wine. The ring survived the crash intact, but not her heart.

I'd love to have a big bottomless martini. I could drink and drink but never get drunk. A martini is a triumph of elegance over pleasure. It's an acquired taste. The martini is a drink that people revisit because they can't believe that it is really as unpleasant as they remember. Each time I expect it to be better than it really is. And each time it is so surprising to be reminded of how truly awful it is. Rather like love.

She was so goddamned young. We were all young. I saw her get married. Lady Di. Soon to be a princess. The long carriage ride. The crowds. That moment when she stepped out of her chariot. She was so demure and sweet and so fucking young. And weren't we all? Weren't we all so fucking sweet and young just from looking at her? And hopeful. She fucked up Charles' name during the vows. I was there. I was outside, in that crowd. Thousands of us. We were all pressed together, stuck together, pressed up against the metal barriers. But no one was rough. We were all in it together, waiting with one breath held in so tight. The carriage came. She stepped out. The dress was what we saw first. That dress came billowing out of the carriage and it flapped and waved and just kept on coming. The train on it was so long, it went for miles. It floated right past me, right by where I was standing, pressed up against the metal barrier.

A little piece of it caught on the metal and tore off. It ripped. And she turned, she looked at me, her little face surrounded by all of that big silky dress. I felt like it was me going to walk into that church. She was me. I was her, in that moment.

I designed my own wedding gown to look like hers. Much more modest, of course. And when I was going through the divorce I'd think, well, this can't be happening. It's all supposed to be Prince Charming and happy for fucking ever after, right? Sometimes I'd wonder, what's she doing now? Throwing herself down a bloody staircase.

The night she died, I watched it for hours, the image of that twisted car in that tunnel. I waited and waited for her to climb out, to give me a sign.

I didn't save my wedding gown, the way some do. I saved the piece of lace that tore of off Lady Di's dress. I gave it away, gave it to the woman I met at the clinic. Bernadette. The one who told me it must be so nice to be a feminist. This because I screamed at some nurse for telling me to turn off my cellphone. This because I had my Notebook. She said, "That's not a notebook. That's a computer thingy. A notebook is a scribbler."

Do everything you can, I told them. I don't care what it takes. I don't care if you have to kill me to do it. What kind of a real estate agent will I be? Nobody wants to buy a house from a one-breasted wonder. People will spend all their time trying to figure out which one I had cut off. They'll spend all their time trying to beat a hasty retreat because the bad luck might be contagious. Who wants to date a one-breasted-wonder bitter spinster with bitchy little wrinkles all over her top lip from smoking? Because that's my future, I told them. That's my future if you don't save my breast. So do it, I told them. Do it. Save my breast. The rest of me will follow.

I'm a Cancer. That's my sign. As in the constellation. As in the Tropic of Cancer. As in a Tropic of Cancer growing in my breast.

What qualities do you enjoy in a woman? That's what I like to ask men, when I first meet them. Are you a leg man? Or are you a breast man? The love of my life did not love me. He loved my breasts. He always told me how beautiful my breasts were. Long after he stopped being interested in me as a person, he still loved my breasts. It got so I hated to hear him say it. I wanted long conversations about life and feelings and philosophies. What I got was, "You have amazing breasts." "Thanks," I'd say. "I grew them myself." He saved his important conversations for other people. Other women. Women with less-impressive breasts.

"Chemotherapy is such a long thing," Bernadette said. "And cancer is such a fast thing." She felt sorry for me. She asked me to pray with her one day. I said, "Fuck that."

Ann Landers said that a woman should take a pencil and put it under her breast, then let go of the pencil. If the pencil falls then you don't need to wear a bra. But if you let go of the pencil and it stays up, then you are sagging and you'd better go buy a good support bra.

I wasn't ever really her friend, although she told me I was. I don't have many friends. Any friends. She irritated me with her stories of her Granny and her teacup and her fixation on the old Pope. My Lady Di story trumped her Pope and I told her so. The Pope is a misogynistic old fart, I told her. One day I fainted in the bathroom, in the clinic.

When I came around she was lying on the cold linoleum with me, keeping me company, she said. We lay there for a while, imagining that we were lying at the centre of the universe and the world even now was orbiting us and us alone, two little bald-headed suns, aglow from radiation and skin stretched too tight over aching bones.

I saw her once more after that, when I went back for my six-month checkup. She was parked in a wheelchair outside of X-ray, reduced to the size of a fragile child in the chair, bundled in a hand-knitted afghan, all eyes and wispy hair looking up at me, looking up at me in my designer wraparound dress and red high heels. Looking up at me in my smug glory of survival. Looking up. I took the piece of lace from out of my bra, from behind my prosthetic tit, and pressed it into her hand. I don't know why. We never spoke.

It left a big space behind, for such a little thing. Who will love me now? Fuck. Now I'll have to rely on my winning charm and sparkling personality. Fuck. But the thing is, I feel so very light, since they took it. So very light, like I could float away just by taking in a deep breath. I could float away, effortless as a gown in the breeze, without hooking onto anything. I drink my Martinis and toast being the one who survived the crash.

Ode to a Nurse

There's a memo came down from admin late last week. They don't think it looks so hot for the nurses to be standing outside the hospital smoking. Smoking can kill you. So can the stress. I smoke so I can cope with the stress. If I quit smoking the stress would kill me. I encourage the patients not to smoke, but I don't really mean it.

Maybe one of these days I'll go get a soft job down in the States. They treat nurses really well down in the States. The pay is good and the weather is fine. I could work in one of those private hospitals where women go to get their facelifts and their fat sucked out. They get their boobs done too. I could even get my own boobs done, if I wanted, if I was in Florida, working with one of those fancy plastic surgeons. I'd get a nice new pair. Not big. No bouncy *Baywatch* tits. Nice and modest and demure. They'd come with a warranty and a money-back guarantee. If anything went wrong with them, I'd trade them in for a new pair.

So they send down this memo from admin saying that it doesn't look so hot to see me standing outside the hospital smoking. I sent them back a memo saying if they give me a raise I'll go smoke in my Porsche like the doctors do.

My patients love me. They tell me I'm a regular Florence Nightingale. Florence in the battlefield, that's me. Miss Nightingale was smart. After she was finished tiptoeing through the trenches, she went off to nurse the wealthy elderly. The rich old guys who just want someone to talk to and a nice cup of tea. Sweet.

Five years ago I was working in Emerge. I was burnt out. I had to save my sanity. So I transferred. I wanted something more stable. Something more uplifting. Some place where I could really make a difference. That's how I came to Oncology.

Nurse, Nurse, oh Nurse. That's all I hear. Nurse. Nurse. I'm thirsty. Nurse. Nurse. I need my meds. I need, I need, I need.

I've got a kid at home. She's home doing exercises, like the old, "We must, we must, we must increase our bust." I told her straight: be careful what you wish for. Those little buds could be dangerous to your health.

People always want to know. They always ask. Are you a cancer survivor too? The answer is yes. I've survived it. I've survived it hundreds of times. I've survived it for every woman who walked out of here alive and for every woman who didn't. Mostly for the ones who didn't. I used to feel really guilty for being the one with the healthy breasts.

Nurse, Nurse. I'm in pain. I need to see the doctor. I need, I need, I need.

Cancer is an ugly sneak. It's a hungry hawk. It hides out. It waits until it thinks the coast is clear and then it pops its ugly head out again.

To mastectomy. Or not to mastectomy. That is the question for a lot of them. But not the only question. What's a girl to do? Does she Lumpectomy with Radiation? Or doth she Mastectomy preserving the underlying muscles and the nipple with a combination of Chemo Cocktails? Or doth she Radical Mastectomy, chop chop, both sides, double whammy, lose the nodes and the arm muscles and the chest muscles? Lose the works with a whammy combo of Chemo and Radiation? What kind of a menu is that? Whether 'tis nobler in the mind to have the poor tit suffer the slings and arrows of outrageous fortune. Or, by Mastectomy, end them. Euthanasia for the breast.

I've got a bra museum in my closet at home. The bras left behind after the surgeries. I save them. Bustiers. Corsets. Full support. Light support. Sports. Strapless. Criss-cross. Push-ups. Cotton. Silk. Lace. Nursing bras, starter bras. Gel bras. Cross your heart bras. Wonder Bras. Merry Widows. All made to encase and hold a little mound of disposable flesh. So many women giving birth to their own three-pound breasts, little breasts, dissected and thrown away while the bras remain intact.

When there's nothing left for them to throw up, I give them water. When there's nothing left to throw up, I give them ice. When there's nothing left to throw up, I give them my arms to rest in.

To Demerol, or not to Demerol. No bloody question there.

I just worked my regular 12-hour shift. Before that I worked another regular 12-hour shift. Before that I worked a regular overtime 12-hour shift. And now I can't shift anywhere because they've got me hooked up to a pager. I can't call in sick because I'm the one on call. So if I do call in sick they'll call me in to go on call for myself. I don't know if I'm coming or going. I go out one door and I see myself coming back in. Who says you can't be in two places at once? I'm torn in two. I am my own clone. I'd go up to the third floor and check myself into psychiatric but they're shorthanded up there too. I'd end up doing my own shock treatments.

I'm going to quit, I think, quit the job and then the pills. I want to ship out for parts unknown. Strange parts, new parts, any parts but body parts. Pamper the aging wealthy, nurse them through their facelifts and tummy tucks and liposuction. I'll go some place where I have a name. Not just "Nurse." And when my own time comes I'll have had so much collagen and Prozac, I'll be the finest looking corpse ever laid out for a wake. If I'm lucky, I'll have myself as my own nurse.

I'll say goodbye to no one. I'll call no one. I will follow up on no one. I don't want to know what becomes of them. I don't want to know how they faced the dying of the light. The truth is not my business anymore.

Talk to Me

I was hibernating in my St. John's home on a rare summer evening off, tucked up on my ugly comfy sofa, surrounded by books and my two magic cats. Rain streaked the windows and it was too humid to cook, making it the perfect time to indulge in take-away noodles. My son Jon was just upstairs in his bedroom, so of course I needed to ask him if he'd like something to eat as well. I thought about getting up off the cozy lumpy sofa and disturbing the Zen combination of myself, my books and my cats. I thought about shrieking Jon's name at the top of my lungs to get his attention. I looked at the telephone sitting on a table all the way over on the other side of the living room. And then I reached into my purse, pulled out my cellphone and called my son on *his* cellphone. He was not a bit surprised to be getting a call from his mother who was sitting mere yards below him. We talked, during which time he put me on hold twice to answer call waiting, but he text messaged me while he was on the other line so I wouldn't feel lonely. (I dislike phone e-mail because I'm nearsighted and I can't pick out the tiny little letters on the keypad. Plus, I don't know any of the slangy shorthand used in text messaging, so I wind up laboriously spelling out complete and lengthy sentences that cost a fortune per inch.) While we were speaking, Jon also took a call on the land line in his room, and with a phone held to each ear conducted two separate conversations with the ease of a maestro. Jon's phone is even more evolved than mine. His cellphone is a headset. There is no phone with his phone. There is nothing to dial. He "dials" the number by giving the headset voice commands. It also has GPS, Facebook, a built-in video camera, digital camera, and 73 other functions.

My own cellphone is tiny, thin and slippery. It's called a BlackBerry even though it isn't black. It's burgundy. It trills when I get a phone call, chirps when I have a message and buzzes whenever I receive an e-mail. It never rings when I want it to and always rings when I can't find it and have to hunt for it in the bottom of my purse. I'm afraid of it. It has 43 different functions, but thus far all I know how to do with it is say hello. Once I accidentally pushed a wrong button and activated the voice command component. A strident female voice publically shrilled at me to "Say a command!" for five minutes before I figured out how to deactivate it. I think my fellow grocery store shoppers at the time thought I was into some strange S&M. Or, more likely, they've learned to appease the voice command goddess and give her important commands to execute. "World peace!" "Stop global warming!"

I swore I would never own a cellphone but that was before I started working many months of the year as artistic director of the Grand Bank Regional Theatre Festival. There is no land line in my Grand Bank apartment. I felt lonely and uneasy being out of reach of my family and friends, so I went to the local Home Hardware and picked up a cheap phone and a prepaid phone card. At first I vowed to use it sparingly, only when I was out of town. I was stingy with my phone number. I used it to check my voice mail in St. John's and to call my son. I was smug. But night after night of seeing it sitting silently on the coffee table of my out-of-town apartment, I caved. I became a promiscuous and prolific cellphone user. Hence the designer BlackBerry.

Was there ever a time when I wasn't available to the world for every second of every day? I am nostalgic for the times when answering a phone call was like opening Cracker Jacks. Who could it be on the other end? A surprise was in store every time the phone rang, not like today with caller ID and custom rings to take the mystery out of everything. I fondly recall the olden days when being a stalker meant I could call my ex-boyfriend up at three o'clock in the morning to see if he was home and hang up in his ear when he answered, secure in the pre- *69 world. I am forced into the truth every day. Lying is no longer an option. ("I didn't know you called." "I lost your number." "The line was busy." "There was no answer.") Cellphones have become the new smoking: no place is off limits, people don't care who's exposed to it, and normally sane folk become nervous and grumpy if deprived.

Privacy is obsolete. My most intimate confidences to my best friend are shared with continuous interruptions of calls, pages, updates and e-mails. "Oh, hi Fabe, yes Berni was just telling me about her gynecological thingy..." Was it ever normal to leave the house and be inaccessible for a lunch, walk or play? I sat in a theatre recently and watched in horror as the lady sitting in the row ahead of me not only answered her cellphone using her "day" voice, but had a conversation while the rest of us tried to focus on the struggling actors. "Oh yes, no not much, at a play right now, it's all right, not as good as I heard it was but there's a reception after so there's free booze." I myself have been in the throes of acting greatness on stage only to hear the horrible downloaded rap-ring-tone-music-sample emanate from the audience. Perhaps we would be better off recording live theatre on our multi-functional cellphones and playing it back later when it is more convenient. I would suggest the only revenge would be for an actor to take a call in the middle of a play ("Hi, oh, nothing much, just in the middle of the third soliloquy") except I am reminded of a recent dress rehearsal when a cellphone did ring on stage. A musician had been using it to download music files.

Last night I was holed up in my Grand Bank nest, curled up on my out-of-town version of the saggy splendid sofa. I was surrounded by my laptop, the TV and the cellphone. The e-mails were coming fast and furious, the phone was vibrating its way across the table. There was a time when work stayed at work and did not follow me home to jump up and down if I didn't answer every call or acknowledge every message. The sun was sliding gently into the ocean the way it likes to do out here in Grand Bank. The wind was warm, the way it rarely is out here. I walked out of my apartment and over the road to the pebbly beach. I crossed the pebbly beach and climbed the Head, a small hill that overlooks the ocean. I sat on top for a long time, thinking about everything and nothing at the same time. I heard a chirp, a trill, a buzz. Oh rats, I thought, and reached into my pocket, where yes indeed I had unthinkingly slid the burgundy BlackBerry. But then! What did I behold? A message on the screen of the phone. *Out of service range.* The chirp had come from a robin, the trill from a gull, the buzz from a bee. They demanded no reply, asked for no commands. If I wanted to speak to another human being I would have to walk quite a distance to do it, much farther than climbing a short set of stairs. It felt ... familiar. Like life before. There is one more thing I am going to learn about my cellphone. Where the off button is.

A Slight Delay

Good afternoon, ladies and gentlemen. Welcome aboard the inaugural flight of Dense Air. My name is Bernadetta and I will be your flight attendant, mechanic, baggage handler and co-pilot for today's journey. Up there in the cockpit you can see our pilot for today, Bob. Bob is also our sanitary engineer, first officer and bouncer. Wave, Bob! As a matter of fact, we're pretty proud of our Bob. Bob is a very recent graduate of Her Majesty's Penitentiary Rehabilitation & Retraining Program for Lost Causes, a very innovative and prestigious initiative. He is the first graduate of the *Flying for Dummies* course. He was the only one who served enough time in the Pen to qualify for the flying hours, which only goes to show that behind every cloud there is a silver lining. By the way, please make sure you keep your purses and wallets in a secure place at all times.

I'd just like to take a moment to tell you that we here at Dense Air care more about you than any other airline. We are not just employees of Dense Air. We are all bona fide owners and shareholders. Not only that, we built this aircraft with our very own hands. Please excuse the sawdust. And please excuse the fact that I am screaming at you. Bob was supposed to install the intercom system but he got tied up trying to fix the knob that came off the throttle.

You will notice that your seats are already in the upright, locked position. They will remain that way. They will not move at all. Not unless the super glue hasn't dried yet. The cushions for the seats are on order but I think the Phentex Afghans are cosy. You will find a piece of rope attached to each side of your seat. (The armrests are on order too!) At this time we ask that you take one piece of rope in each hand and tie a knot securely around your waist. In case of any change in cabin pressure while we are in flight, we ask that you immediately retrieve the paper bag that is Scotch-taped to the ceiling directly over your head. Put the paper bag over your mouth and breathe deeply. Please do not use these paper bags if you experience motion sickness. There's a box of plastic Ziploc baggies glued to the seat in front of you for that purpose.

Most airlines no longer provide life-jackets in case of emergency and we are proud to be no exception. In the rare instance that we have to make an emergency landing on water, you will find an inflatable rubber ducky underneath your seat. It may look really tiny but when it is fully inflated (a process that takes approximately 15 minutes, depending on your lung capacity), it fits snugly around your middle. Plus, it is yellow, so it is easy to spot if you happen to be bobbing up and down in the middle of the Atlantic Ocean. Also, every rubber duck is numbered, so the first survivor to reach dry land qualifies for a Dense Air travel voucher valued at $10.

There are three emergency exits on this aircraft. One to the rear, one to the front, and one through the ceiling if you're skinny and can fit through the seam where we ran out of siding. We like to think of it as our very own sunroof! Also, it provides ventilation for when we light the propane stove for our in-flight hot beverage service. Tea and coffee are standing by, and for a modest surcharge your beverage is served to you in a delightfully quaint Carnation milk can. The label costs extra. And we will be passing around a pot of boiled beans and bacon. Be careful because the handle gets mighty hot, and please lick the spoon before you pass it along.

We will be getting ready for takeoff momentarily, just as soon as we finish strapping the last of the luggage to the roof. And, for the person who is travelling with the Great Dane, no worries! We've got his crate securely duck-taped underneath the right wing of the aircraft. Just a reminder, though, folks. Please note that according to the fine print on your ticket, same-day arrival of your luggage is not guaranteed and in case your luggage is lost, misplaced, arrives in a different city, or falls off while in-flight, we disavow any and all knowledge or responsibility. When you examine the fine print on your ticket you will also be interested to note that there is an aircraft exit charge applicable upon arrival at our destination, regardless of whether it is the destination of your choice or not. At that time you will have to pay a cash fee of $100 if you want to get off the aircraft. Otherwise you will have to face the wrath of Bob.

You may have observed that this aircraft is not equipped with any television or movie screens, no headsets, earphones or special listening channels, no complimentary newspapers or heated cloths, no phones, no satellite service and no magazines. However, once we have reached our cruising altitude I will be performing for you, live and in person, my one-woman show entitled *My Seven Year Peri-Menopause*. There will be a service fee of $15 each for this performance. Bob will collect after the show.

Sit back now, and relax folks, we're about ready to take off. This is Dense Air Flight 001 now departing for Whitbourne, Goobies, Marystown, Clarenville, Gambo,

Gander, Grand Falls, Badger, Deer Lake, Corner Brook, Stephenville, Codroy Valley, Isle aux Morts, Port aux Basques and the Gulf of St. Lawrence, en route to Fort McMurray. In the event that this aircraft is not permitted on the ferry there will be a slight delay in our arrival of approximately three months. In this day and age we realize that you have choices when flying, and we appreciate that you decided to go with Dense Air. As our corporate slogan says: We may be slow, but we're cheap." Thank you and have a great trip! Hold on tight now, we don't actually fly, we taxi the entire way and aren't these highways a disgrace!

The After-Dinner Entertainment

"Whistle them down," the old man says to me from behind. "Put your lips together and whistle them down to the water."

I'm standing on the waterfront of St. John's Harbour, having just walked downtown from the swanky glass hotel where I was the After-Dinner Entertainment. The horizon is streaked with subtly moving ribbons of green, a slow-motion kaleidoscope gently caressing the night sky.

I left the hotel in frustration. I got tired of waiting around for the person who promised to try and locate the person who last saw the person who may or may not have my cheque, my performance fee. My contracts always stipulate that I get paid on the date of my show, but many times this clause is treated as an arbitrary obligation, even a nuisance.

There are different types of After-Dinner Entertainment. One is your bona fide Celebrity Appearance. A true Star gets paid thousands of dollars to show up and be themselves, only more so. These true Stars can sometimes be confused about what gathering he or she is being paid to grace, or which city they are in. This person can sometimes fall asleep at the head table, or get names wrong, or sometimes appear to be even less so than they seem on TV. The audience doesn't mind. I aspire to this.

I do not command the same fee as my better-known colleagues. In fact, it was suggested that since this was an international gathering of luminaries I do the event for free, seeing as it is such great exposure. I long ago learned to counter this suggestion by proposing that the person on the other end of the phone go to his or her job and work for free for a week, for the exposure.

At other times the After-Dinner Entertainment is a "person of interest," paid to speak on a particular topic, such as Global Warming or Financial Matters. This person is well known in his or her field of work, but not a celebrity. They are esteemed, which is better and longer lasting than stardom. I, sadly, am no expert in anything.

One time I was the After-Dinner Entertainment for a well-known public service organization, but it turned out I was to perform after the After-Dinner Entertainment, the main event being a stripper flown in especially from Montreal. She had blonde pigtails and appeared on stage dressed up like Little Red Riding Hood, wearing a silky red cape and a short swirly skirt, both of which were flung into the audience shortly thereafter. We shared a dressing room where I tried very hard not to stare at her naked bits. I found myself functioning as her secretary/chaperone, answering the door and screening the constant flow of men who wanted to inquire if she "needed anything, anything at all!" I kept my clothes on for my own performance, ignoring the audience pleas to "Take it off! Take it all off!" I coveted the red cape. She gave me a large red feather instead. She used it to play peekaboo with some of her naked bits when she was on stage. I stick it in my hair when I perform Welfare Goddess.

The old man steps from out of the shadows to stand beside me. I see he is Native, fine spiderweb lines across his face, a hand-rolled smoke between his fingers. From where we stand we can see the steady stream of car lights motoring up Signal Hill. It looks like half the city is heading up

there for the concert of light. I'm too preoccupied to wonder if I should be wary of the stranger. The mortgage is due
tomorrow and I've no cheque to show for my night's work.
The bank will not be amused or even tolerant. I know this
from the time I tried to explain that the mortgage was late
because the cheque fell down behind the fridge of the
Secretary-Treasurer of the group who hired me. The
Secretary-Treasurer promised to get it to me just as soon as
she had the fridge moved for her spring cleaning, "next
week some time."

I am the opposite of the naked After-Dinner
Entertainment. I get paid to put clothes on, costumes, hair-
nets and frowsy dresses, funny glasses, badly styled wigs,
garish shoes. I get paid to show up as little old ladies, fish
plant workers, eccentric housewives. I am the sort of After-
Dinner Entertainment known as the "local flavor," an artist
of modest merit. We are professional artists (theatre practi-
tioners, they call us now) who earn our living through our
craft. We like to be given leftovers to take home.

One time I was the After-Dinner Entertainment for a
gathering of realtors. When I arrived for the show at the
ritzy Yacht Club I saw a sign advertising me as, "The other
one from Codco!" I guess Cathy Jones was busy that night.
I have never been a part of Codco but I did not dissuade the
gathering of this notion for fear it would delay my cheque.

Sometimes I am asked to sit down to dinner with everyone beforehand, but I can't because I'm always very nervous. I wait before the show in various hotel rooms, both
chic and tawdry. I wait in chilly washrooms that are in
assorted stages of cleanliness. I wait in hotel kitchens while
servers carry trays of hot food back and forth, where I am

sometimes mistaken for the help who is supposed to serve coffee and dessert. I often eat with the kitchen staff after the show. They are universally kind, candid about which of my routines work the best.

One time I was the After-Dinner Entertainment for a retreat of breast cancer survivors. They had a little ceremony during their dinner at which every woman walked up to a blackboard and wrote down the number of years, months and days she had been living with the disease. They paid me promptly with a cheque, a pink bejewelled broach, and a floppy hat which I wear in the summertime. I've never seen anyone else demonstrate such an appreciation for time, and for being timely.

I've been the After-Dinner Entertainment for judges, teachers, nurses, crown prosecutors, forensic specialists, heavy equipment operators, firefighters, grocery store chains, career counsellors, politicians, scientists, health and safety experts, hotel managers, conventioneers of every kind. I've performed in halls, ballrooms, theatres, bars, clubs, tents, hotels, motels, fields and once in someone's living room. I've been heckled, hit on, picked on, lauded, loved, ignored, applauded. Once someone threw a rubber chicken at me. Once someone gave me a bonus in the form of a bunch of gift certificates at a local Home Hardware store because he had heard me say my house needed painting. Once I met a woman whose husband was in jail because he tried to kill her by stabbing her, and she told me I had made her laugh. Once I did a show in a bar where nobody, absolutely nobody, listened to me because a recent runner-up from Canadian Idol was moonlighting as the bartender while he waited for his CD to be released. I receive the spontaneous outpourings of stories, confidences, jokes, the gifts of key chains and pens that accompany the cheques. I am that rare species whose livelihood depends on the unlikely fact that somewhere, someone at some point decides that after a lengthy day of meetings, after a liquid-filled cocktail hour, after a heavy meal at the end of a long evening, there must be After-Dinner Entertainment for the weary multitudes. I am it.

A taxi pulls up on the street behind the waterfront, and the lady from the City jumps out, waving an envelope and clutching a Styrofoam take-out container. "Oh there you are! And here's me looking all over creation for you. Don't you want your cheque?" She leaves in the taxi, off to Signal Hill with some of the international luminaries.

The old man sucks on his hand-rolled cigarette. The smell of the leftovers, crab in a pastry, wafts up from the Styrofoam container. I open it and offer him a plastic fork. He shakes his head, no, and gives his cigarette the flick. I do know enough to recognize the Northern Lights when I see them. I haven't seen them very often. I was born in North West River, but I was little when we moved to the Burin Peninsula, although I like to say that I have dual citizenship status: blood red ochre runs through my veins, my bones are Labradorite.

The Northern Lights lounge across the sky in a series of careless poses. "Whistle them down," he says again. He strolls to the edge of the dock and begins an offhanded eerie whistling. I begin to eat and watch while the Lights dance down and flicker off the water. The mortgage will be paid. The food is still warm. The After-Dinner Entertainment tonight is exquisite.

Just a Quick Note

Hi, love. Just a quick note to say that I hope you're doing well and taking care of yourself. I'm so glad we had the chance to talk and clear the air last night/early this morning, even if it was through your screen door. At the time I thought it was pretty darned unfriendly of you not to let me in, because we always said we were friends first and foremost, and always would be no matter what. But now that I've had an hour and a half to reflect upon it, I can see your point about the Rottweiler, and me naming it after your new girlfriend even though it's a boy doggy. And I didn't mean to insult your new girlfriend when I called her "Dogface" to her face. I meant it as a compliment because I love dogs so very much, and you and I always talked about getting a dog together. Anyway, it was nice to finally meet her. I think her lazy eye is actually kind of cute. So many people have told me that her face has got a lopsided look to it, but now that I've seen her in person I will defend her to the death. I've mailed you some literature on treatments for lazy-eye disorder, because she does not have to live with that squint. Still, inner beauty is a wonderful thing and I'm sure she's got tons of that.

Anyway, as I said, this is just a quick note to say hi and to offer to pay for the patio furniture that Melanie chewed up. (the Rottweiler, I mean, not your new girlfriend.) Canadian Tire is having a patio furniture sale, so if you like, you and me and Melanie (the Rottweiler, I mean, not your new girlfriend, although she can come too if she wants to) can go look at some. It won't be the least bit strange for me, even though you and I always talked about buying patio furniture together at some point. In fact, there's no reason why we still can't, seeing as we're always going to be friends no matter what. New girlfriends come and go but friends are there for you forever and ever. Plus, I've still got your Canadian Tire credit card.

So, this is just a quick note because I don't want to take up too much of your time. I know how hard it is to have to do open-heart surgery when you've been sleep deprived. (Remember all the nights we stayed up late, watching the NHL playoffs and having sex every time someone scored a goal?) It was really sweet of you to hear me out the way you did, and to not call the cops. I also think that the new motion-detector security system you've got installed in your backyard is super cool. And, boy, I guess you and me both are happy to know that it works so very well! That's why I was prowling around in your backyard at midnight with the Rottweiler in the first place. I've been very concerned about your safety, what with the rise in the crime rates and all. So, whew! Am I ever relieved. I'm so glad I could reassure you about that.

If I had more time I would write you a longer note, but I am definitely going to take your advice and get on with my life now, and accept once and for all that our split is permanent. By the way, did you change the password to your voice mail? I'm only asking because a friend of mine mentioned that she left me a message on your land line and I couldn't retrieve it. Perhaps you could check and see if there are any messages on your voice mail for me. I keep giving out your number by mistake as my contact number. Just habit, I guess. If you want to give me your new cell number I can give you a call at work and we can arrange to get together so I can return your house and car keys. I somehow came away with them last night. They must have accidentally fallen into my purse when we had that little tussle over trying to get the screen door open. Or, well, closed. I could tell by the look in your eyes that you would have let me come right on in if Melanie (your new girlfriend) wasn't there. Does she really sleep in that nightie? I remember your mother telling me once that only sluts and whores wear red nighties. I thought she looked just adorable, which is why I was taking pictures with my cellphone. If you or she would like to see how adorable she looks, the pictures are posted on Facebook. She's pretty flat-chested for such a big girl. I only mention it because I remember you telling me how much you loved voluptuous women, and I wouldn't be your friend if I didn't point out that she's built like a pudgy boy. I wouldn't want people to start thinking you were turning gay or something.

I wish I had more time to write a longer note cause I remember those cute little text messages we would send each other all day long. I don't want to deprive you of knowing how I am and what I'm thinking. In fact, it's even better to write each other now that we are just friends, because we can tell each other everything without anyone getting jealous. For example, you could tell me about the fact that you bought Melanie (your new girlfriend) a gold necklace for Valentine's Day. I was coincidentally shopping in the same store at the same time you were there. You probably didn't notice me because I was wearing a red wig and big sunglasses at the time, and standing behind the gift card display. Plus, I didn't want to intrude. (You see! I CAN be subtle!) I went ahead and bought Melanie (the

Rottweiler) a gold-coloured collar. I draw the line at getting Melanie (the Rottweiler) a red nightie but I did e-mail you a few pictures of Melanie (the Rottweiler) and me in the bathtub. Eighty-seven photos, to be exact, so if you get a file that slows down your system while it downloads, be patient! It's worth it! But my point is, you can go ahead and tell me about the necklace you bought for that hussy (just kidding!) and the romantic weekend for two at the B&B you put on your Visa. (Yikes, I forgot to mention I had your Visa statements redirected to my house in case there are any old charges on there I owe you. Sorry!)

Before I sign off, I meant to tell you that I have a new boyfriend who is madly in love with me. I don't mean to catch you off-guard or make you jealous or anything like that. My new guy is just adorable. He's really handsome, and I hope you won't be offended if I rave that it's great to be going out with someone who has all his own hair. Thankfully, he is not one bit put out by my constantly talking about you. And he doesn't mind the life-sized tattoo I have of your face. It's on my back, did I mention it before?

Now that I think on it, these little notes are a wonderful way of staying in touch. I will write you another later on today and one tonight before I go to bed. It's so much easier than the phone, seeing as we keep getting accidentally disconnected every time you answer one of my calls. And e-mail is just too impersonal for the personal confidences that arise between friends. The only drawback is that snail mail takes so darned long! I just thought of something. I can just pop on by and slip it under your door. That way you will get it as soon as you get home and you won't have to spend the rest of the day wondering how I am. Better still! Seeing as I happen to have your house and car keys, I can just let myself in and put this on the kitchen table. Actually, why don't I take Melanie (the Rottweiler) out for a walk, pick up some groceries and some wine, let myself in, make you a yummy dinner, and I can give you this in person! Won't that be nice?

Play Me Home

I'm a fisherman's daughter, his only girl, come to him late in his life. My brothers get to go out on the water. It's expected. But I am not allowed. Him and Mom being fearful that the sea will try to claim me back.

It is impossible to tell from looking at my old black and white baby pictures that there was anything at all different about the way I was born.

Everyone wanted to pay money to take my snap when I was a baby. A lot of people travelled a long way to see me in person, too, and offered Mom and Dad money if they could have a peek at me. A newspaperman traipsed all the way out from St. John's to write up an article for the "Believe it or Not" section of *The Sunday Herald*.

Baby fetched up out of the water in a net. A miracle found in amongst the fish. A mermaid with no tail. *Believe it or not.*

Why not believe it? Some babies are born with cauls, the thin membrane of good luck stretched across the face, ready to be saved as an heirloom, or sold as a treasure. Some babies come out with a full set of teeth, already talking. Babies come with extra fingers, or with two noses. They come as Siamese twins, they come as changelings, they come with whiskers, seventh sons come to seventh sons, they come and come, meant for another world than this perhaps, but they come all the same.

Dad showed me the net that carried me up out of the water and told me how he hauled it up with his own hands. I was born, little sister, little daughter, little mermaid, covered in fish scales, stinking of cod, the flopping cod that kept me alive and warm as they thrashed and twitched around me. The very air that killed my fishy brothers and sisters was the same air I gasped for, my lungs filling up with the salty wind as my Dad hauled me up from out of the ocean.

Mom, being a midwife, has birthed all kinds of souls into the world. They come, new souls inside of little wrinkled bodies. They come, old souls happy to have new lungs, howling, greedy for another chance to live. They come and come, sometimes too soon, with the lungs not ready to take on the weight of air, and they expire, fish out of water. I came, not with gills, with lungs, fished from out of a sea-drenched net.

Mom and Dad wouldn't let anyone take peeks at me for any amount of money. Dad set the geese on the fancy news-paperman so he had to turn around and take the boat all the way back to St. John's again, with the arse ripped out of his shiny pants. Dad said he wasn't going to have me on display like what happened to the poor Dionne Quintuplets up there in Canada, the Government taking them from their family, making them grow up on show.

My Dad lifted me up from out of the net and passed me over into the arms of my Mom. He played us all home. And that's how my life began. With one deep breath.

Our house sits in the middle of a big meadow, overlooking the ocean. I never went out of sight of the sea, until the Bullet. It took my Dad and me ten hours to make the trip up the Burin Peninsula, to Goobies. Ten hours in a sweaty car, sucking in the dirt that flew up from off the road. Then it took the Bullet another twenty-four hours to get to Corner Brook. The waiters in the dining car wore white gloves and called me "Miss." The Conductor asked me: "Where are you going in such a pretty dress, Miss?" So many miles passing between me and home, passing beneath my feet. The Newfie Bullet and a one-way ticket to The San.

They stick you in a bathtub as soon as you walk through the doors. As if you're dirty. Dad hugged me goodbye and that was it. Next thing I'm naked as the day I was born, sitting in a bathtub with a nurse looking at me. Twenty years after I came up out of the net, I'm on display after all, people peeking at me, having to get my picture taken over and over, with the all-seeing x-ray, stewing in a strange soup of chemically flavoured water.

Nothing in the cavernous room except the single bathtub in the centre of the floor. I was wishing I could feel my net underneath me, to have something to hold, to know that someone could haul me out if I got too weak or fainted. The Nurse brought me a cup of tea, in a real china cup and saucer, with a bag lounging inside the hot water. The bag had a string tied to it, draped over the side of the cup. I tore the teabag open, to let the tea leaves out. I poured them all into the tub with me. A mermaid with no tail, steeped in her own tea.

I get a needle in my hip every day. Thirty pills a day. The size of golf balls. Streptomycin. Needles in my lung. Taking out my ribs. Trying to outrace the galloping consumption. How does anyone ever recover? At least it's better here than it was in that old place in St. John's, with a mouse man going around setting traps. People die in the night. After a year, my lung did not heal. It had too many lesions on it. It was trying to grow a set of gills. They cut me open, gutted me, took it out. They tell me my fiddle days are over. Now I have to think about every breath I take. I can hear music whistling through my one lung. Whistling from the effort of taking on the work of two. Taking on the heavy air.

It takes breath to play the fiddle. Breath is where the strength comes from. Strength to take in the heavy air. Strength to play them home. The body is built for two lungs, but, luckily, music is light as a feather. The one left behind plays the other one home.

At home, I go out into the meadow to see if Dad is on his way back in from off the water. He keeps his cor-deen in the bottom of his skiff. My brothers go down to the wharf to help him haul in his load. It's funny. You'd think we'd feel queer about eating fish. But we don't. We always bless the meal: "Lord, thank you for this fish we eat, and thank you for this fish what gave us Jade. Amen."

And every evening, when it's time for my Dad to be coming in, I put on my best dress and go out into the meadow. I play, and then I listen. I play until I hear the sound of his cor-deen floating in from across the shore. And that's how we know he's made it safely home for one more day. No matter what the weather. The one left behind plays the other one home.

He bought a new cor-deen with the money that came in from the Government. He says he will never admit that we are a part of Canada, and Confederation is a queer thing, what with checks coming in, left, right and centre. And here he never knew what "retirement" was, never mind knowing that he is, in fact, supposed to have been "retired" for long ago. He's got a new reel he made up. He calls it "Jade on the Train."

I wake up in the morning and I see an empty bed on the ward, where a person lay sleeping only the night before, the sheets stripped off of it, the night stand emptied out. I think about the Dionne Quintuplets sometimes. Coming five at a time, as if they knew they'd have to keep each other company forever.

I hope for a nice boy who will like me for who I am and not expect too much. Two lungs and one heart, is how we're born. But anyone looking at a picture of me now could never guess that there is anything at all different about the way I am.

Once you've been here for weeks, that turn into months, that turn into years, it doesn't seem possible that you will ever get to go home again. But stranger things have happened. Like a baby being fished up from out of a net. My mom was down on the wharf, pregnant with me, raking in the fish, when she went into labour. She slipped on the fish guts, but like all babies who are ready, I came anyway, heedless, headstrong and hearty. I popped from out of her warm body. I slid along the slimy wharf and fell right down over the side of it. Right down into the dark, cold water. Down, down, down, coming to rest in a net of living cod. Dad pulled me out and lifted me up. Little sister, little daughter, little mermaid with no tail.

Little girl with one lung, taking her first breath. Dad will take the Newfie Bullet to come get me when the time comes. We will be served china tea cups with hot water and tea tied up in bags. We will untie the bags of tea and let the leaves swim free.

I have a friend. He's a boy. He's downstairs on the second floor. We take turns, visiting each other in the evenings. To say goodnight. He likes me for who I am. I've written Mom and Dad about him, of course. He only has one lung. On the right. I only have one lung. On the left. So, between us, we've got two lungs, and two hearts. Enough to have a family, we think. Enough to take on the weight of air, and anything else that life on dry land has to offer.

He plays the cor-deen. The one left behind plays the other one home. A person with one lung can have babies. I read it in the "Believe it or Not."

Mary Magdalene

Station One: "Live And Let Live" Afternoon Delight AA Meeting.

Sorry. Sorry. Sorry. I don't mean to be trespassing. If I'm trespassing then please forgive me my trespasses for having trespassed against Ye. *Mea Culpa, mea culpa, mea maxima culpa.* How are Ye doing? How's everything with Ye?

I think there's a bit of broken glass on the go. I'm all sparkly. Is it different colours? Is it different colours? *Is it?* Is there yellow? Is there? Is there blue? Is there any blue? I miss blue.

I'm good. Don't touch me. I'm not cut. I'm not cut.

"Alcoholics Anonymous." Ye are the Alcoholics. I was looking for Ye. I hope I'm not having a blackout. If I am, Ye must be having a blackout too.

This is a queer sort of underhanded miracle to be pulling on somebody. I was chasing the wind. I heard the tin whistle. I heard it. It led me right to the front door. Listen. Listen. Oh…it's gone. But, they've got the front doors of the church all locked up. To keep the vagrants out, they say. But now I'm thinking, it might be a trick to lock all the alcoholics in. There's a sign says, "Alcoholics please go around to the back." I said, I'll go in, but I'm not going around the back. It's the front way or no way. And then! Wooooosh!

Sorry. Sorry. I didn't mean to call Ye alcoholics. The sign says "Alcoholics" but it also says "Anonymous." So, I don't know. Does that mean you *can* say alcoholic or you can't say alcoholic?

I'm soooo shiny. Do you have a mirror on you? Do you? Do you?

Alcoholics Anonymous. That's right. This is safe. This is sanctioned. Cause, this friend of mine took me out drinking one time so she could talk to me about my drinking problem. I only went because it was free booze. And she's not even a friend at all; she's only a bag lady, camped out, lives two vents down from me, stole a bottle and had no one else to talk to. I don't even remember her name so she can go frig right off. Sorry. Jesus knows I'm a little shit disturber. Anyway, I know God wouldn't laugh. But there's no need for her to be telling me I'm an Alkie. She should have said "Alcoholic." She's mean.

Look at all the food! Oh, you're allowed to feed the Alcoholics. There's no stopping the miracles today. If I'd known there was grub I would've come long ago.

Oh, sorry lady, were you giving a speech or something? Betty. Is it? Betty. Oh. Ooh. Betty…. So this is what you do in here, is it, Betty? Sit around and talk. That's nice.

How do you frigging *talk* if you don't have a drink? What's to talk about if you can't drink? Cooped up in here. You can get out, though, right? I'm not locked in, am I?

We met outdoors, in fields and caves and beaches. Jesus didn't like temples. I've got my own Vent across from the Eaton Centre. It's in front of the Urban Outfitter. You could meet there. Or better yet, you could get your own Vent. Stay clear of that new spot they've got cleared off on the corner of Dundas, though. You think it's the perfect spot to lie down for the night until they turn all those fountains on.

You've got to feed the crows, though, if you're going to hang out on my corner. But you don't have to worry. I am the only one who knows how to cross the crows, so you won't get bad luck. One for sorrow, two for joy, three for a girl, four for a boy, five for silver, six for gold. Seven for a secret.

How it works. Oh. Instructions. Here are the twelve *steps* we take. Number One: We admitted we were powerless over alcohol.

I admitted I was powerless one time. Went underground. Became anonymous. I still got persecuted for it, so I think you might be kidding yourselves.

Twelve steps, steps steps steps. I can't go doing any steps. My feet are killing me. There's *fourteen* frigging Stations of the Cross up-stairs, got them painted on them big stained glass windows, trying to look so pretty. People crawl around on their hands and knees making the Stations—that's two more than your twelve steps—and they still don't get nothing out of it except the knees scraped off themselves. So, how do you know those are the right twelve steps? Who says? They could have twenty Stations of the Cross up there. I'd still be pissed off because half of them are wrong.

"God grant me the serenity." A Serenity Prayer. I don't know that one. I don't pray anymore. I used to know all kinds of prayers one time. *Misereatur vestry omnipotens Deus, et dismissus peccatis vestries, perducat vos ad vitam aeturnam.* Look at that! Just falls out of my mouth, like so many rice crispies.

Listen. Listen. Listen. Sirens. What time is it? Is it…is it…it's not…it's not…

Betty. Betty, is it, Betty? Can I have the lend of some change from out of your collection plate? Sorry for trespassing upon Ye. Oh, and sorry, but one of those big stained glass window Stations upstairs got broken.

Station Two: "The Happy Hour" AA Group.

That was wicked! That was wicked, Betty. No, yes it was. Yes it was! I know God wouldn't laugh. I mean, if I was looking at you now, without just having heard your…whatsit…your speech, your "Drunkalogue," right? I'd never guess you could have sunk so low as that. Lying, cheating and stealing. That's three commandments worth right there, Betty! I gotcha beat! I'll see your three commandments and raise you two, Betty! And I can't remember the half of what I'm doing. But your daughter likes you again now, so. That's nice. That's a real miracle. Oh. So, we're having cake now, right?

Well, make no wonder you were so good with the cops as you were yesterday.

She was great with the cops.

You were, no, yes you were, Betty. That's my greatest fear, you know, getting locked up, locked in somewhere, blue-arsed fly banging my head off a brick wall. They were going to haul me down to the Station for breaking that stained glass window Station upstairs. I *told* them what happened to that window. God sneezed.

Oh. Oh! And then Betty goes, she goes, "Now then, officer! Do you really think that huge window was twisted in by this little creature?" I thought that was a good one, because, all creatures great and small, right? And then she says, "How dare you make assumptions!" And there's me, picking the glass off me as she speaks, but I didn't do it.

If I was up on charges as many times as you've been up on charges, Betty, I'd be good with the cops too. No, really, you were great.

You'd never think she got in a car and drove over some-body just to see if the brakes worked.

Gimmie some of that cake. Got to feed those crows.

Nope, cops don't mess around with Betty. Cops don't mess with people who've got nice things. I used to have lots of nice things one time. Gold chains. I had an emerald the size of an egg. Rubies dripping off me like blood. Oh, and the gorgeous big wedding band I had. It was real gold. It had engraving all around it and everything. But I lost it.

I used to love to stand naked in front of a big mirror, nothing on but all my jewels. All the jewels men gave me through the ages. I'd be coated in them. Stand and stare. Touch the jewels where they touch me and tingle all over. Shimmer. Glow. Sparkle. The men are dead and gone for long ago. Princes. Poets. Paupers. One Plumber. So much for undying love.

I've got no earrings, though. I'm not allowed to pierce my ears. I may not puncture my own flesh, lest I want to trudge through all eternity with the ears rotting off my head. Thou shalt not covet thy neighbour's earrings. That's my tenth commandment. I'd love to have that many holes in me, earrings galore, wind playing through me like a tin whistle. Put the Holy Ghost right to shame, I would.

Jesus said, "Let he who has ears listen." And Betty said the exact same thing to me! "Just come in and use your ears and listen." So that's why I'm here. And that's why I'm not talking. And, look! Look at this! She gave me this, the twenty-four sobriety chip.

What colour is it, Betty? Is it a colour? I suppose Ye've all got tons of these. Twenty-four hours sober and you get a prize. A piece of plastic.

Shit, Betty's got twelve years, think you'd give her a frigging car or something. Or, the Nobel Peace Price for sobriety. I'm showing this to the frigging cops if they try to pick me up again. Oh yeah. Betty told them she's my sponsor. Well, she is *now.*

I told you I'd come to the flipping meeting, Betty. Are you happy now? I'm here! I'm not going to sneak out the back door. Is that the back door? Because, twenty-four hours is one thing. But do I desire to stop drinking altogether? Because that's a prerequisite for joining up, right? I was thinking about that. Every frigging day I say, I'm not going frigging drinking. I say, I'm only going to drink on weekends, but then I start the weekend on Thursday and I finish it up on Tuesday. That only gives me one day a week to get sober, so I say on the weekdays I will only drink in the evening, and then I start the evening at four o'clock. I say, I'm only going to drink on odd days but on even days I feel odd, so I drink then too. I say, I'm only going to drink on good days, but no day is good if I can't have a drink, so then I only drink on bad days, which makes the bad days good, so I drink on the good days too. So. I just want to get it under control. So I can say, I am a social drinker. So I can have a few drinks, like anyone else. So, I'm more interested in doing the express line version of AA. More like the six-step version. Get a bit of, you know, sleep instead of those damned blackouts. Oh, a blackout doesn't mean I'm passed out, sleeping it off, you know. I'm up walking around in my blackouts. I'm in a total eclipse of the mind, the feet on me dragging me around like Lazarus. I'm exhausted from walking around with the First Stone in my shoe.

Oh. You're not here too? Do you remember me?

Betty. Betty. Betty. "There is another standing here who shall not taste of death till they see the Son of Man coming in His kingdom." Malchus. What happened to you after…? You've got yourself tortured! You need a drink! Water, no more wine for you. You've lost your gumption. Stuck in here with the Catholics like Christ among the lepers. Do they let you keep Kosher? Do you still keep the Sabbath? Do you pray, Malchus, do you pray? I've been mixing my meat and my milk. I've been mixing my p's and my q's. Nope. Nope. Nope. He's not in his right mind. I'm going to be *his* sponsor! I know he looks like a plant, but who among us can rightly say what we were before we came here?

Station Three: Mary Ministers to Malchus at the A.A. Listener's Meeting.

Let us all put our hands together for Malchus! Congratulations, Malchus. That's wicked, Malchus. Let's hear it for Malchus. He made it through twenty-four hours of sobriety.

You know what that means, Malchus. You get the twenty-four hour Sobriety Chip. Me too. And one for good luck. Also, I brought you something. Some of the hair of the dog that bit you. Miracle Grow.

I didn't always drink, if that's what you're thinking. Jesus started that, when He changed the water into wine that time. One sip. *One* sip and you knew you'd never rest until you could taste wine as sweet as that again. You'd slit your own wrist and drink your own blood if you thought it tasted half so good. But it isn't your own blood you want to be drinking. "Take this and drink of me." But He knew. Jesus knows. I *never* drank before that.

You and me, we're in the same boat, Malchus. We're all in the same chalice.

Betty, they've got me pissed off with what they did upstairs. Nailed those boards over that broken Station. Nailing up the Station where He was nailed to the cross. You know that's not right. Why don't they board up the Stations that are wrong?

Station One: that one's right. He is condemned to die. Station Two: He carries his cross. He did. I wouldn't want to see the likes of it again. Had Him hauling around a cross like a camper trailer on His back. Me walking behind Him like a bridesmaid, nothing to do except count the steps steps steps.

Station Three: He falls the first time. He fell and that was the downfall of you, Malchus. You said to Him, "Get up and get off my doorstep!" Jesus stood and said to you, "I am going and you shall wait till I return." Station Four is: He meets his afflicted mother. Station Five: Blah-blah. Six is: Veronica wipes His face with her holy napkin. Bullshit. It wasn't *Veronica*. Oh, and He fell the second time and I was thinking, get up get up get up get up, so we can finish. And you want to know the Station that *really* pisses me off? Station eight: He speaks to the Holy women of Jerusalem. It wasn't women. He spoke to a *woman*. A woman rendered *anonymous* by some near-sighted baggy old Gospel writers. Just a bunch of jealous green-eyed men. Trying to get me into bed all the time. The things they write about me. All those books. I don't read them. Just making money off me.

Oh, and then they tore the clothes right off His back. But I didn't look away. Not like some. I was in my right mind. I looked Him straight in the eye. I think that's when my blackouts started. There was one crow on Calvary that day. One for sorrow. The sky went the colour of pitch.

They take His body down. It's still warm. My hair soaks up the last of His blood. I suck it out, just to get the taste of Him. I never get a grey hair after that, not to this day.

He really did all the things people say He did. He really did walk across the water. I was there and it wasn't beautiful. It made Him seasick. After He died I was in the garden. There were *two* crows. One for sorrow. Two for joy. And when I crossed the crows He appeared in the garden too. I thought He was the frigging gardener. He would have been a beautiful gardener. He spoke to me but it's no good asking me what He said because I don't remember anymore.

Poor Malchus. You're in a total eclipse.

He's in a total eclipse of the mind. The wandering Jew who wanders no more. Immortal doesn't mean invulnerable, you know.

You and me, we got that in common, too. Any little thing. Any little thing denied and it's all you can think about. One more journey. Earrings.

Station Four: Thursday "Pass It On" AA Meeting.

Sorry, sorry. Shit. Sorry. I'm late. I'm late. Now don't be coming up to me and trying to get me to breathe on you. I've had nothing to drink today. I only had a bracer for four o'clock. I've got it under control.

Hello. My name is Mary M. That's me. My name is Mary M. and I enjoy a scattered drink.

Malchus, here you go, buddy. Little hair of the dog for the maggoty plant. Malkie with the Alkies. Sorry I missed you yesterday, Malchus, but I was busy.

"He who has a mind to understand, let him understand." You've got a mind, Malchus. You've got to get your gumption up. You've got to get your feet in underneath of you again. Your roots.

I need a coffee in the worst way, thanks. Oh, I like that room you got me, Betty, but I've got no flipping kettle yet.

Oh, it's a good room Betty got me. It's not much bigger than my Vent, but I don't mind. It's got a clean bathroom. I have a brand new shower curtain with fishes and loaves all over it.

Is it blue, Betty? It's shiny. I'm used to a good bathroom. I'm used to the bathrooms at the Eaton Centre and they are very high quality. So, I need a good bathroom. Although I'd like it better if it had a hand dryer and a thing that squirts the soap out.

Betty gave me a good present too. She goes: "My first year of Sobriety I took up hooking." And, I'm thinking, "What?" Then she's hauling out all her rugs, she's got 340…how many? Three hundred and forty-seven rugs. Ye should see the likes of the one she gave me. She copied the pattern off the Shroud of Turin. That dishrag they say has got the image of Christ imprinted on it. I says to her, My dear, I know you thanks Jesus you're sober, but I'm not going wiping my feet off in his face.

I wish I could have a smoke, but I suppose you can't smoke in the church. I just don't feel my day is started unless I've had my Whore's Breakfast: a cup of coffee and a smoke. The Last Supper was on a Thursday, you know. That's why Thursday is the best day for happy hour. "He came to pay the debt He didn't owe because we owed a debt we couldn't pay." And there you have the beginning of bar tabs and expense accounts. Course, you can't even smoke in the bars anymore. You've got to go outdoors and you know that's not right.

Because, there are very specific rules for women who want to smoke, you know. Or I should say, for *ladies* who want to smoke. It's how a woman smokes that shows if she is a lady or not. A lady can only smoke while she's sitting down. A lady can smoke while she's standing up, but only if she's at a party and not if she's all by herself. She can smoke only if she is standing up, inside, at a party, surrounded by a crowd of people. She would never smoke while standing up alone all by herself in the bar of a strange hotel. A lady never smokes while she's outdoors, never smokes while she's walking, and never ever while she's standing up walking around outdoors. Only sluts do that. And a lady only smokes if she is having an alcoholic beverage. A drink. Or *when* she's having a drink. Or she must have a drink whenever she smokes. Whichever suits the day. A lady never lights her own cigarette, of course. Hopefully the same attentive gentleman lights all of her cigarettes for her. Ideally, that would be her husband. A lady doesn't accept lights from just anybody. A lady never lights her own smoke because that would make her look desperate, and a lady is never desperate.

And there are very special rules for women who want to drink. Or for *ladies* who want to drink. It's how a woman drinks that shows whether or not she is a lady. A lady buys all her own drinks. Or, hopefully, all her drinks are paid for by the same attentive gentleman. Ideally, that would be her husband. She never accepts a drink a strange guy, no matter how lonely or frightened she is. A lady never buys rounds for the bar, never buys drinks for strange guys, and never talks to strange guys while she's drinking. Only sluts do that. A lady can drink as much as she likes, as long as she's elegant about it, pays for it herself and doesn't talk to strange men. A lady would never order a whole bottle of wine just for herself. Especially not one with a screw-top. A lady sips her drink as if she doesn't really want it and as if she has all day to enjoy it.

A lady can light her own smoke as long as she's all by herself in the bar of a seedy strange hotel, drinking alcoholic drinks bought for her by a bunch of strange guys whose names she can't remember because she is elegantly yet certainly ossified loaded drunk out of her mind and no longer gives a fuck.

Station Five: "One Day At A Time" AA Group.

Okay. Betty told me to get my ass here today and chair this meeting. Malkie is helping me out. Just a minute. Just a minute.

You need some of the hair of the dog that bit you, Malkie. Miracle Grow and vodka. We've got to wrap this up by four o'clock.

Now I'm supposed to read from the Big Book? Is it blue? "Rarely have we seen a person fail who has thoroughly followed our path." I'm supposed to read *all* the Twelve Steps? Well, I'm not. Ye have heard this all before. Hello. My name is Mary M. and I drink like a fish. Except, now I've quit. I know you've all heard by now what happened two nights ago. I fell off the wagon, or, like you say in AA, I had a little slip. If Betty hadn't come and got me there the other night out of the lockup, I guess I'd still be in there now. I came to in the tank. There was 32 women in there and one toilet in the middle of the floor. You know that's not right. I don't know what set me off.

Oh yes I was in the this bar the Nervous Nun, you remember where the Pope Joan used to be on Parliament? And everything is all sparkly. Lights on the booze and lights in the mirrors. There's a half empty wine bottle on the table next to me. See, that pisses me off. People are always leaving half empty drinks around. Now you know that's not right. That's a waste. So I went over to the table and I got it. And there was this lady watching me, going blah-blah, looking down her nose at me and pointing and waving her hands, flashing this gold ring. I don't know what came over me. I ran over like a savage and grabbed her hand and bit that ring right off her finger. I know God wouldn't laugh. I'd laugh myself if it wasn't so funny. I don't remember throwing up all over her Dolce & Gabana. Betty told me that. I don't remember passing out. But I *do* remember that was *my* genuine real gold wedding ring she had on, the one with the engraving on it. The one I lost. I thought it was.

My life is going to be different, now that I've quit drinking. Again. It's amazing how different life can be, thanks to Ye and this program. It's a world of difference, being sober. It's as different as night and day, up and down, black and white, queer and straight, it's as different as drunk and sober, that's how frigging different it is. Well, for one thing, what's different is, before, I drank. Now, I don't. So now, I'm "not" drinking. So that's different. It's all I do. "Not" drink. I spend all my time at it. Before, I spent all my time drinking. Now I spend all my time "not" drinking. It's a full-time job. I'm crucified with all the not drinking. Well, number one, you can't drink. At all. You can't celebrate, commiserate, demonstrate. I am prostrate on the altar of sobriety. I shudder to think where I'd be today if I was still drinking. Drunk, passed out, fallen down, necking in some bar with some stranger. But now that I don't drink, my God. My chastity, my sanctity, my soul is saved. I can hold my head up high. I'm really enjoying sobriety.

The thing is: it's only been forty-eight hours since my last drink. So what the hell am I supposed to do with the rest of my life? Never mind the rest of eternity. What am I supposed to do with the rest of *today*? I mean, I've been on the go since six o'clock this morning, and I washed my face and brushed my teeth and I've washed my hair three times today. I fed the crows. I've got the DT's and I drank twenty cups of coffee on top of that and I've smoked twenty-seven and a half cigarettes, and yes I lit them all myself. I went for six walks. I'm after reading all the frigging Steps twenty times. I did step Number Four today. I made a searching and fearless moral inventory of my self.

I've got morals, you know. Morals are very important to me. Even though Ye all think I'm a whore. Well I'm not. I'm not. I wasn't a prostitute. They made me out to be one and I did fool around a bit, but that was *after*. I whored around but that doesn't make me one. A lot of times I never even charged any money. And, I could have. I'm good. But I gave up men. It just took me a long time to figure out that a heavy blanket would've been just as good.

I'm a very very kind person. I did wash His feet, that part is true. Washed His darling feet and dried them off with my own hair. He saved me. That part is true too, but then I saved Him right back. He came crawling on His knees to me, crying, "Save me, save me, save me." He says, "I want to lie down like an ordinary man and rise up like an ordinary man." So I let Him. And we did. And this wind roared right through us, played us like a tin whistle.

He really liked my ears, but I don't. They stick out. Is that the time? Is it? Oh, shit, it's quarter to four. I've got to go. Got to go. Oh. Wait a minute? Do I get a chip for chairing the meeting? Have you got a Chair-the-Meeting chip? I like this one, it's different. What's that one, six months? Can I trade in my 24-hour chip for a six months? I don't understand why I can only say I've got one day of sobriety. I had two sober days last week, and yesterday and today, that's four. How come we can't pin our new sober days on to our old sober days? I'll never get twelve years at this rate. And that means, Betty, if you have one little drink, then your twelve years don't count no more and you've got to go back to the one-day chip? That's not fair. Okay. We close with the Serenity Prayer. God grant me the… something to know the wisdom. Blah blah. I gotta go. I gotta go. I gotta go.

Station Six: Mary Magdalene's Etiquette for Young Ladies at the A.A. Speaker's Meeting.

The first glass of wine is not the best. The second glass of wine is the best. The second and tenth glasses of wine are the best. The worst are the first and the ninth. The first is the worst of all. It isn't enjoyable at all and is best gotten through quickly. There are too many lies, too much shame and guilt in the first glass of wine.

You know, I'll just have this one. Just this one and then I am on my way. I…on my way…I used to go places…journeys…you know. I've got places to do and things to go and people to be. I'm only going to have the one. I really shouldn't even have this one; it's so early in the afternoon. Well, it's almost afternoon. Another couple of hours and it will be afternoon. A lady does not have her first drink until the afternoon. Definitely before four o'clock. But just this one, just this once. I can handle it.

But the second glass! The bliss! So delish! So full of freedom and euphoria! Oh, what the hell. I can do all that stuff tomorrow. I'm on top of things. I deserve a break. I feel good! And tomorrow I won't drink at all. It's nearly afternoon. The day is shot. I worked for a whole hour this morning. A lady knows when to give herself a break.

The ninth glass of wine is bad though. It takes experience and faith to get through the ninth glass. Oh God. I'm sho drunk. How did thish happen? I didn't mean for to get thish drunk.

Make it through the ninth, though, and you're on to the tenth and you get your second wind. It's all clear sailing, clear skies. You get so drunk you sober up again. And after the tenth, things are fine until the nineteenth glass of wine. The twentieth to the twenty-sixth is a real test of poise. The twenty-seventh is pure love. And I live for love. So. The worst glasses of wine are the first, the ninth, and the twenty-sixth...do you need to hear it again? I can go over it again with you later. The best glasses of wine are the second, the tenth, and the twenty-seventh. Although, a real lady never counts. Because you know what they say. One drink is not enough and a thousand is one too many. So. No going overboard tonight. Tonight I will drink socially, like a lady. I'm only going to have twenty-seven glasses of wine. That's okay. That is my limit. I can cut myself off after that. A lady knows her limits. Twenty-seven glasses of wine and a lady switches to brandy.

Station Seven: "The Twelve Steppers" Meeting.

Don't blame your daughter, Betty. I asked her to buy me that can of Glo-in-the-dark blue spray paint. I know I can't see what the colour is, but I told her to get me the shiny stuff. I told her I wanted it for my room. Okay, that was a lie. That's one commandment's worth right there. Commandment number eight, thou shalt not bear false witness. But I never defaced anything! I was doing them a big favour upstairs. I drew it on the plywood they boarded up the broken window with. Look on the bright side! I was in my right mind when I did it. I do not have to be explaining to Ye what I did or did not do with the spray paint. I'm two thousand years old. The frigging Church is not going to kick Ye out. Ye are the only ones who come in regular anymore. Sure, the church is half empty up there all the time now! Pews and pews and rows and rows of beady-eyed saints staring down at nothing. Don't get mad at Betty. Betty.

I ran into this friend of mine yesterday. I remembered her name! Sooze. No. Sandra. It was Rachel. Shit, I was calling her Sooze and Sandra the whole time. Anyway, I asked her how her husband was. "Dead," she said. What happened to him, I asked? "The drink," she answered. "He died of the drink. Drink is all he ever did on the end of it. Morning noon and night. Drink. The doctor told him. The priest told him. I told him. Everyone told him that the drink was going to be the death of him but he wouldn't listen. Then one night he got loaded drunk and fell in the harbour and drowned. He got himself full of the drink and fell in the drink. He died of the drink." It's too bad no one ever mentioned AA to him, I said. "AA!" she said, "My God, he was never that bad!"

And I say to myself: I'm not that bad either. Although, some evidence is as hard to ignore as, like a fish in the milk. Such as when I wake up in the middle of the night and can't move for the bruises. Thinking, I'm living like a whipped dog, crawling under the veranda to lick my wounds, creeping out into sunlight, forgetting about the damn cars.

Station Eight: "Hand in Hand" AA Group.

I've got a hobby now, thanks to Betty. She told me how to lick that demon drink. Get a hobby. Betty knows what she's talking about. You should see her house! It's better than a gift shop. She doesn't invite just anyone over. Rugs, you know the one she gave me, that's what she did in her first year of sobriety. The second year she made angels out of clothespins. One hundred and twenty-three of them all over the windowsills. I know she gave you all one. She's got 32 popsicle-stick replicas of the CN tower. Built to scale. Seventy-three little coke can windmills all over her front lawn, they're gorgeous.

Yes they are, Betty! I'm that jealous, the wind gets inside them and plays them like a tin whistle.

You should hear it. She's got 79 of those toilet paper thingys, you know, you make little hats for the toilet paper rolls. She gave me this one, it's a Snowman.

You have put me on the path to creation, Betty. My hobby is: I collect plastic forks. See? I get them out of the garbage cans at the Eaton Centre. You put them like this and this and take a tube of crazy glue, got to watch out for that crazy glue, and glue the forks together. Put some pretty paper on them and you've got a fan. A lady always carries a fan.

My other hobby is: I took up watching TV. I've got a brand new second-hand TV. Someone put it out with the trash. I told you people are always wasting things. Gets two channels on it. It's got no picture but the sound is all I care about because my room can be very quiet. But it's nice though. Last night, three o'clock in the morning, this Infomercial comes on for Jesus. This show filled with testimonials from people, people who are kind of sort of not quite anybody, semi-almost-famous people. And they all say that they found Jesus and now they are closer to being famous. All you need to do is call! Don't delay, phone today. 1-800-Call-Jesus. So I traipse out and down the stairs and get to the phone booth and I haven't got any money on me. And I try to call collect but you can't call Jesus collect. So then I've got to go panhandle for a flipping quarter. Got a quarter, spare a quarter, got a quarter. Some good Samaritan gives me a Toonie and then it's, what do I look like? A frigging charity case? I only asked you for a flipping quarter. Change a Toonie, got change for a Toonie, trade a Toonie for a quarter. I dial the number and it rings, it's ringing and ringing and ringing. And I get a recording. It says, "You can't call here from there".

Shit, it's four o'clock. Why is it four o'clock? Betty. Betty. It's four o'clock. I know I'm your cross to bear, Betty. I knows I'm the big camper trailer on your back. But it's four o'clock.

Station Nine: Mary, Mary.

Betty won't answer the frigging phone. I called her fifteen times and I let it ring long enough in case she was in the bathroom or doing one of her hobbies. Does Betty have a secret life or something? She's always there, she always said, call anytime. I just want to tell her, I can't sleep in that room anymore. I'm going mental in there. It's too quiet. I can't think for all the quiet. I miss my Vent. I don't want her to worry. I'm going back to my Vent. It's way nicer. But you've got to stay here, Malchus.

And I've got to tell her I'm not going up there with her kowtowing to that baggy old priest. I scrubbed off the spray paint, that was enough. I didn't mean to get her in trouble.

Well, if it isn't the afflicted Mother of Christ. How's this for a veil of tears. *Ave Maria, gratia plena.* Mary, you've met Malchus. The wandering Jew who wanders no more. Malchus, you know my mother-in-law? Most recently seen in an oil spill under an overpass in Detroit. The Lord be with thee. Well, the Lord *is* with thee, isn't He? *Your* statue in all the churches. *Your* mug plastered from one end of creation to the other while I'm just plastered. You look good. Had some work done? What do you want? Another miraculous appearance in a potato? Or on a nacho? Weeping tears of blood to drive some poor fool mad?

Oh, she's really good, Malchus. Comes on all hazy in a ray of sun, and the next thing you know you're running around, trying to dig up a Holy Spring.

Look at her. Look at her. She's the genuine article. An A-list celebrity. I bet you'd get *your* own infomercial. Oh yeah.

Oh yeah. I knows God is not laughing. I'd laugh myself if it wasn't so funny.

Look at you. Look at her there with her little white feet.

Did Ye have to turn me into a joke? Got me turned into a joke and a drunk and a whore. I'm not a drunk. I've been sober for three days. In a row. And that's not counting my other days. But I miss my vent. I miss my black-outs. I miss coming to and a whole century's gone by of things I don't want to remember. Today I remember yesterday and tomorrow I'll remember today and the day after that I'll remember the day before. If it keeps going this way I'm going to remember everything. It's all going to come back in a great two thousand-year-old flood. The seven demons He cast out of me. That time I anointed Him with oil. The way they came by the thousands to hear Him. The sound of His voice.

His voice in my ear. "Let he who is without sin cast the first stone." His empty tomb.

I can't think for all the remembering.

So many steps steps steps. I told Ye. I told that Betty. I can't be doing no steps. You should see the feet on me.

Station Ten: "This Too Shall Pass" AA Group, Church Basement.

Hello, everyone. My name is Mary. Mary Magdalene and I am loaded.

Yes yes yes. *That* Mary Magdalene. There's no need to whisper and nudge. I've got eyes in my head, you know. I can see. I've got big sticky outy ears on the side of my head. I can hear. Yes yes yes. You know me from the Bible. I am a real A-list celebrity. I am She. The Hidden Martyr. The oldest living relic. The Holy Grail. His Dearly Beloved. Patron Saint of the Penitent. Yes yes yes, I *have* had a drink today. I accidentally went into a bar and had twenty-seven glasses of wine. And then I started on the Bloody Marys. But the good news is: I gave up eating meat! Although, define *a* drink. *A* drink can go on for an eternity. If there's anybody else here tonight who is still *active*, see me after. We can pool our resources. Right, Betty? Where the frig is that Betty? I frigging called and called and called, but no frigging Betty. I suppose I can't call there from here.

We should all go out for a drink. Whattaya say? We're all drunks. Where are all the sober people? In the bars, that's where. What's the point of having all the alcoholics holed up in crappy rooms in the basements of churches while all the sober people get to go to the bars and drink their asses off. I came to out of an alcoholic black-out this morning and thanks be to God I can't remember anything. All I know is: I am the burning bush. I open my legs and I part the red sea. "Let he who is without sin cast the first stone." Well, guess what, folks? Somebody threw it. Since the beginning of time I have walked with that rock in my shoe.

Every step that I take is with the First Stone. I'm the walking stigmata. I'm the pillar of salt.

Jesus! Jesus! Are you taking phone calls tonight? I'm done! I'm done! I'm not waiting anymore! Go ahead! Go ahead! Come on if you're coming! Call down the floods. Tell the heavens to weep. Come on, walk on the water, I'll build you an ark! Slaughter the lamb.

Come on! Come on! What the frig are you waiting for! Jesus Christ have mercy on me Lord have mercy on me Christ have mercy on me Jesus Christ have mercy on me Lord have mercy on me, Christ have mercy on me, Jesus, have mercy on me have mercy on me mercy mercy mercy mercy have mercy on me, Lord, my Lord, have mercy on me, have mercy on me, have mercy on me Lord make speed to save me a sinner.

I need a drink. Anyone got a drink? Want a drink? I need a drink. Where's Betty? Fuck you, Betty.

Station Eleven: "Take it Easy" AA Meeting.

So, there we are, me and Betty, in that room she got me. And she's giving me this placemat, it's her latest hobby, she's crocheted it herself and it's nice, only, it's got this weird pattern on it. And I says, what is that supposed to be, Betty? And she says, "I'm crocheting you your very own Stations, Mary. Thirteen13 Stations of the Magdalene. That's a picture of you flying through the window the first night you came to us. I'm going to do you and Malchus, and you stealing sobriety chips on the sly. I know you can't see the colours but they're going to be pretty." And I says, Betty. It just looks like…a blob to me. And she says, "Yeah. That's so you can make it out when you're loaded."

I miss her. Do you miss her too?

At the funeral today I counted seven crows. One for sorrow, two for joy, three for a girl, four for a boy, five for a fortune, six for gold. Seven for a secret that will never be told. That's so queer, cause I told her one of my secrets. What the deal is with four o'clock for me. She knew: it's a bad time of the day. Betty knew it. She held me down enough times. She knew. She knows. After Jesus died, when I saw Him in the garden that time. He spoke to me. He asked me a question. "Will you wait for me, till I come back?" And, I said yes. And then He kissed me goodbye. And when I opened my eyes He was gone. That's when every colour in the world turned to grey for me.

I never got to tell Him. I never got to tell Him to His face. Sure you'll always be inside of me.

That was four o'clock in the afternoon. Every day at four o'clock something happens to me. Every day at four o'clock

Jesus kisses me goodbye all over again. I don't know how I'll get through it without Betty. Better than a heavy blanket, Betty was.

Something I did not tell Betty. That day on Calvary, when they had Him up on that evil cross, He turned his head to look for me, His Dearly Beloved, but I didn't look Him back straight in the eyes. I looked away. I was the crow on Calvary that day. One for sorrow. It was me.

Join hands for that Serenity Prayer, now. Betty likes that one. God, grant me the serenity to...how does it go? To accept the things I can't change, the wis...oh yeah, the courage to change the things I can and the wisdom to know the difference.

Rest in peace, Betty.

Station Twelve: The Penitent Magdalene

Blue!

Station Thirteen:" Keep It Simple, Stupid" Recovery Group, Church Basement.

Hello. My name is Mary Magdalene and I am an alcoholic.

I've been having so many adventures lately. I can't tell you. I was in the park this morning, having a whore's breakfast, that's a cup of coffee and a smoke. So I figured I'd go ahead and have a whore's bath, too, in the duck pond. That's what you call it when you just wash the stinky parts.

Look. I can see, I can tell. Blue…green…orange, Betty liked orange.

You know what else I did? I pierced my ears. I used the First Stone.

Ye can have this. And this too. This is the cloth I wiped His face with. That was me. Keep it, in remembrance of me.

Do you like my ears better with earrings in them? They're Betty's. Her daughter tracked me down, came by my Vent last night and gave them to me in person. Asked me if I wanted to come over for dinner on Sunday. But I had to say no. Cause, we're going on. Me and and the crows and Malchus. We're going on a big pilgrimage. The tin whistle is playing again. The wandering Jew will wander again. And I'm going to walk until I take that final step.

I am going. But Ye don't have to wait till I return.

Listen. Listen.

Beauty Tips for the Vain and Deluded

The day of the kid's birthday I spent the morning squinting into the bathroom mirror. "Not too bad for a chick with a twenty-six year old. I don't look a day over twenty-six myself. People probably think we're siblings. People probably can't believe I'm old enough to have a grown son. People probably think I had him when I was fifteen. No, ten, make it ten. No, that's demented. Maybe I can say I adopted him when I was ten. I wonder if I can ask him to call me Sis." Then my mother called and told me that my son was twenty-five and his birthday had been the day before. She wasn't impressed by the fact that at least I got the month right. I put my glasses on, removing the myopic illusion of youth and beauty. Those aren't pillow creases that are going to fade from my cheeks after a few hours. Those freckles are liver spots. The greys are coming in like weeds and there's a hair growing on my chin. All that squinting has taken a toll. I'm kissing the backside of fifty. I am vain and deluded, but middle age means I must have some sort of built-in reserve of wisdom, somewhere. I've learned a thing or two about how to nurture the Vain & Deluded spirit. It's time to pass the torch. These are my beauty tips for the woman of a certain age:

Reduce neck wattle by constantly craning the neck as if searching for something on the horizon. Very good for posture.

Don't laugh at anything you don't really think is funny.

Pulling the band-aid off quickly is better than pulling it off slowly.

Always wear make-up to go to the grocery store. You never know who you're going to see there. Probably some-one you don't want to see. But they will see you. You can wear your pajamas to the grocery store as long as you are wearing your make-up, except if it is the make-up you applied three days ago. Make it a point to wash your face every two days whether you need to or not.

Sucking on a lemon will remove the red wine stains from your teeth.

Smoking gives you wrinkles. Quit smoking. Drink more red wine.

Quit smoking. Eat more. Better to be Rubenesque than a cadaver.

Pretend your toes are on your thighs and touch them ten times a day. Not necessarily all at once.

Do not fish for compliments. You won't really believe them.

After the age of forty-five be sure to moisturize your feet. In dog years your feet are now one hundred thirty-seven.

Use un-moisturized feet to exfoliate your shins.

Shaving is a seasonal must! At least once every three months.

Do not seek the approval of others. It will give you hound dog eyes.

Always wash your armpits every morning, and anything else that hangs down, like your belly button.

A response for all occasions: Your friend asks, *Do I look fat in this?* Reply: You don't look any different in that than you do in anything else. Your friend asks, *Does this new haircut suit me?* Reply: You can carry it off until it grows out. Your friend asks, *Will you come with me to the six-hour production of* Russian Songs My Mother Sang Me*?* Reply: I would, but I don't want to. (An all-purpose reply, in addition to "I'd love to but I don't want to.") Your friend asks, *Did you like the copy of my new play I gave you last month?* Reply: Mmmhmmmm. I don't really have the words. (another all-purpose reply.)

Never, under any circumstances, stand in front of a three-way mirror. The best mirror to examine yourself in is the one in the bathroom just after you've taken a shower, while it's still all steamy. There is a reason why great actresses of a certain age insisted that the camera lens always be coated with Vaseline.

Let your eyebrows grow together. You will look smart. Plus, it covers the worry lines.

When everyone around you is losing their minds, give them yours. Literally. Give it to them.

Wear all your best stuff all the time. People save their best stuff for special occasions. This is ass backwards. "I can't wear it all the time, I'll wear it out!" Well, yeah! Wear it out into the world and every day will be a little bit more special. This goes for jewellery, hats, scarves and underwear. And never adhere to the "less is more" policy. No one has the right to tell you that layering earrings, necklace, scarf, hat, wrap, cape, skirt, pants and sweater over leg warmers is too much. Does Mother Nature tell the rose bush to only grow one flower?

Some primates groom each other while they gather to gossip and sip cocktails. (Picking nits while slurping on fermented oranges.) Always tell your friends if they have lipstick or spinach on the teeth, ink on the face, the back of the skirt tucked into the pantyhose, if they accidentally forgot to wear pants, if there is gum in the hair, crusts in the eyes, drool on the chin. This is a Karmic responsibility. You must do this even for strangers, even for people you don't like. Otherwise you will return home one day and look in the mirror only to find that you were not entrancingly captivating all day, you were, in fact, walking around with a piece of snot on your cheek.

Marlena Dietrich braided her hair into impossibly tight and painful little braids in order to achieve a more youthful visage: slightly parted lips, raised eyebrows, an attractive deer-in-the-headlights look. You can achieve the very same effect by opening all those bills you've thrown behind the fridge.

Crying relieves the body of toxins and makes the skin on your face puffy, thereby rendering a more youthful visage. (So does drug de-tox.)

Wearing unpressed garments distracts from an unpressed face.

Hot flashes, rage, depression and PMS are caused by Global Warming, which is in turn caused by atmospheric disturbances from satellites and space shuttles. The best therapy for any of these disorders is screaming. Plan your screaming time each day. Shriek yourself hoarse. This works. If you do your screaming at the sky, the energy will be sucked up, and you will also be doing your part toward filling in the hole in the ozone layer.

Don't forget to take the time to stop and smell the kitty litter. If you do not have cats and you can still smell the kitty litter, clean your house.

Outer beauty is how you introduce the world to your inner beauty.

Inner beauty is way more important than Outer beauty. Being Vain & Deluded means being a mass of contradictions.

It is recommended to motorists that they always have an emergency kit in their vehicle, with jumper cables, road salt, spare tire, and emergency flares. Every woman should have an emergency kit in case of a bad day. It should contain a small sample of your favourite scent (your "jump start" into a crappy day), a really good moisturizer (smoothes and soothes the "salt" of tears and aggravation), your favourite lipstick (your emergency "flare"), and one absolutely reliable dress or top that you love, which hides the "spare tire." One piece of chocolate is optional.

Converse with yourself. Out loud. Pretend you are your own best friend. Ask yourself things. Wait for the reply. Out loud. Cry on your own shoulder. Be your own confidante. Be the recipient of your best wisdom. Out loud.

Be 'Big' in yourself. Do not indulge in false modesty.

Trimming your hair will not make it grow faster. Trimming your hair makes it shorter.

You don't need to wear blush. Just masturbate.

Don't squint. It's nothing you want to see very clearly anyway.

Coffee is a vegetable. (It comes from a bean.)

Farting is good. It reduces bloating.

Men "dress" to the right or to the left. It is much the same when a woman decides whether the belly should go above or beneath the waistband. Above the waistband is cool because then it's all pretty much out there for the world to embrace, and you can still fasten your belt beneath and cling to the illusion of a 29-inch waist. Below the waistband is fun, too. Go get a big pair of those mama panties. Make sure the top of your pants is flush with the top of your panties. Just below the breastbone ought to be right.

Do not pluck your eyebrows while looking into a magnifying mirror. As a matter of fact, never look into a magnifying mirror.

Those aren't bags under your eyes. Those are provocative thought-lines filled with intrigue and alluring come-hither angst. The most beautiful women in the world look tortured. Think Catherine Denueve; Greta Garbo; Phyllis Diller.

Yesterday's underwear still counts as clean if you turn them inside out.

Open your door and look outside at least once a day, twice if you're really feeling creaky. If you see your shadow, come back inside. If you do not see your shadow, come back inside. Don't go out unless you're feeling really brave and you're equipped: dark shades no matter what the weather, scarf to hide the lower half of your face, loose top to hide the gut. Even so, you will be immediately recognized and accosted by someone who doesn't like you but who will insist on talking to you anyway and who will drop little "bombs" of subtle insults upon you. Better to stay inside.

If you love someone, set them free. If they come back to you, they are yours. If they don't, stalk them.

If you love someone, tell them.

If you love something, set it free. If it comes back, it wants something. Usually money.

Men age differently than women. If a man gets old and ugly, he can just grow a beard and cover it up. So can we, once the hormones hit. Every whacky chin hair, lip hair or mole hair is nature's way of giving us our very own built-in window scraper. Or barnacle scraper. A way of saying to the universe, "Frig off or I will scrape you with my facial hair." There is a reason why those hairs are stubborn and wiry: to remind us of our right to be here. We will not "Pluck off!"

Ditch your frenemies. Do it.

Validate the person behind the counter. She is us.

When you go to the hair salon, find the person who has really great hair. And then make an appointment with the person who does his/her hair.

Let "As is," be your mantra. People who place ads in the classifieds to sell stuff always specify "As is." Meaning: no alterations, no improvements, no promises, no guarantees. As is. Buyer beware. The world can take it or leave it.

Find at least one thing to admire in the mirror, even if it is on the wall behind you.

Find at least one thing to admire about someone else, even if it is how they are oblivious to their many flaws and shortcomings.

In the insipid, yet iconic, film *Love Story*, the main hippy-dippy character (Ali McGraw) proclaims that love means never having to say you're sorry. This phrase became a mantra for a generation. It still appears on sappy cards, heart-shaped gadgets and furry dolls. It is simply not true. Love means always having to say you're sorry and then apologizing for having been born on top of that. It's what you do when you love someone. I am going to emblazon it on hammers and sell them at the Hallmark stores.

The CBC has an entire series based on the fact that if all women leave town, the place falls apart: men can't function and the kids go haywire. The ads invariably show hapless men trying to diaper screaming babies, or burning supper on the stove. Not only is this insulting to men, but if it is true that women are still the silent slaves who do the drudge work, then we are all deluded. And, clearly, if everything falls apart when we leave, why haven't we left before this? The solution to the world economic and environmental crisis is for women to simply stop and not start again until or unless we get to truly harness our power. If there was a series called *The Week the Men Went*, no one would notice, because women function very well when men are absent. It would not have any of the entertainment value. But perhaps it would have another, more meaningful value: perhaps one too profound for our national broadcaster. For the sake of our true beauty, let us lobby for a day when we all stop. Hmm. CBC could call it: *The Day the Women Stopped.* Kind of like the classic film *The Day the World Stood Still.*

A storm day can be just as good as a trip to the Bahamas. Turn up the heat. Put on your bathing suit. Fill the tub with hot water. Get in the tub with a book and a fizzy drink. Bathing suit is optional, although if there is anyone else in the house it comes in useful when trekking back and forth to the kitchen for more chocolate. If you decide to answer the phone, do so in a foreign language. Pretend you don't speak English. If anyone insists on speaking to you, offer to sell them a time-share in your closet.

In ten years time you will look at photos of you from now, and marvel at how young and lovely you were. Why wait the ten years? Marvel now.

The authentic spirit waits to be seen. The authentic spirit validates herself. Like a parking receipt you get from the parking garage. When you are frustrated or hurt, simply stamp it: validated.

When you get out of bed and you have a bad feeling, get back into bed.

The authentic spirit will not allow herself to be rushed into anything.

The authentic spirit understands that you can never "get" anyone to like you. You especially can never "get" anyone to love you. If they don't "get" you, then you can't "get" them. Even if you think you "get" them and if they only knew you, they would "get" you. N'uh-uh. Get it? Got it? Good.

From the authentic spirit: I recently met a woman who was fishing cod, salmon and lobster from the age of fourteen. She got married at the age of sixteen. She is now fifty-four years old. I asked her what keeps her going. She said, "There's always hope."

Risk is the spice of life. Risk does not cause upheaval. Rather, the opposite. Risk keeps things calm and certain. NOT taking the risk causes us the angst of "What if?" Once the deed is done, the outcome is known, and we move on.

Stare at the sea whenever possible. Except when driving.

Indulge yourself in the very latest spring fashion accessory: crinkle cut French fries! They are inexpensive, yummy, easy to prepare, and satisfy the most discerning palate, espcially when served with that other culinary delight: ketchup. Plus, when there are a few leftovers on the plate for a few hours, they harden, and you can string them and bead them for some one-of-a-kind earrings and pendants. "Nibble" art. You will never go hungry if you are stranded in a snow bank.

Never go on a diet. If diets worked we would all be skinny. Plus, you would have to forego the delights of crinkle cut French fries.

A stranger asks, "You don't remember me, do you?" Reply, "Honey, I can't even remember my own son's birthday."

Be a cheapskate. Cheap cosmetics are just as good as expensive ones. Cheap moisturizers are the same as designer brands. Cosmetic companies do not want you to know that the bottle of Sunlight dish detergent can give you a super clean head of hair in a pinch. If it can cut the grease on your frying pan, you just know it's got to be as good as micro-dermabrasion on the skin.

If you don't wear 80 percent of the garments hanging in your closet, give 80 percent away to a women's shelter. You will love wearing the 20 percent that remains. If you have to lose ten pounds to wear it, give it away. Even if you can't act your age, act your size. Take up space in the world.

Cellulite is nature's Etch-a-sketch.

It's OK to be afraid to try new things. Some people like to go around trying new things and some people like to stay home and read about it. This creates balance in the universe.

Exercise can be a lot of fun, especially when you sit around and watch other people doing it.

It is possible to have too many cats. If you are single, count your cats.

You are never too old to have a boyfriend. Boyfriends can be better than husbands because you do not have to watch them clip their toenails. If the boyfriend clips his toenails in front of you, threaten to get another cat.

A woman of a certain age is knowledgeable about what, exactly, boyfriends are good for. They are good for driving you places, talking, watching TV, occasional but required dates, more than occasional and required love making, and for shoring up your vain and deluded illusions.

The boyfriend of the woman of a certain age is a very lucky boyfriend. The woman of a certain age has worked out what she wants. She knows how all her bits and pieces work. She knows that farts are healthy. She will watch *Hockey Night in Canada* to see what Don Cherry is wearing. She knows that in the dark with our clothes off we are all created equal. Hot flashes mean she is prone to stripping off at a moment's notice.

Lately the counter staff at my neighbourhood Tim Horton's is largely made up of "senior" ladies. Grey-haired seniors that one would more easily imagine at home knitting mittens in front of a cozy fire. I wonder if it is boredom or financial necessity that drives them to serve the madding crowds, the line-ups demanding "double-doubles," and "triple-triples," and "double-extra-triple-triples." They move with ease, endlessly patient, those of us on the other side of the counter reduced to being a pack of mindless pseudo-grandchildren. The woman of a certain age knows that this is, possibly, the future, and leaves a tip.

The kid came along on a stormy night in Antigonish, Nova Scotia. The date was January 5th, 1984. The time was 10.14 p.m. If I could go back now and speak with that overwhelmed young mother, I would tell her that I catch a glimpse of her every now and then, when I squint into the bathroom mirror. I would tell her that she's holding up just fine. The kid is doing well and I bought his love and forgiveness with a belated birthday present of $150.00. I also catch a glimpse of her when I look at him. Sometimes she's there, in the tilt of his head, the blue of his eyes. The vanity, the beauty, just beginning.

ACKNOWLEDGEMENTS

My thanks to: Donna Francis, Janine Lilly, Ed Kavanagh, Joan Sullivan, The Newfoundland Quarterly, Jill Kieley, Robert Chafe, Artistic Fraud, Amy House, RCAT, Donna Butt, Rising Tide Theatre, Kay Anonson, Lois Brown, Andrena Morrish, Jim Payne, the NLAC, Canada Council for the Arts, Lighthouse Productions Inc. and my son Jonathan Lambert Gibbons Stapleton.